The Tree of Resilience

The Tree of Resilience

Seven inspiring women's stories highlighting the eight elements of resilience and strategies on how you can develop yours

Julie Hickton

© Julie Hickton, 2013

Published by Natures Coaching Ltd

A CIP catalogue record for this book is available from the British Library.

ISBN 978-0-9926710-0-6

Book layout by Clare Brayshaw

Prepared and printed by:

York Publishing Services Ltd
64 Hallfield Road
Layerthorpe
York YO31 7ZQ

Tel: 01904 431213

Website: www.yps-publishing.co.uk

About the Author

As an experienced executive coach Julie specialises in helping people be the best they can be at all that they do. Working with individuals who; have a desire to enhance their leadership capability and impact, those who are overwhelmed by what and how to achieve their accountabilities or deal with change, or that are unclear what their future holds and wish to take time to explore their future life and career, or developing their emotional intelligence. She creates an environment where others are able to think more freely that brings challenge, support, fun and often a different perspective. Her role has lead her to support people make changes and create more balance and enjoyment in their lives.

Her work with teams has enabled her to encourage and produce enhanced working relationships through developing trust and a more collaborative approach which has enabled them to achieve more successful results together.

She is inspirational, fun and passionate about helping others to grow and maximise their unique talents and strengths whilst creating balance and enjoyment in their lives.

She has been privileged to work as a Non Executive Director within the NHS where she has been strategic and challenging as well as supportive and encouraging.

As a HR Director she was involved in personal and company change and culture development as well as leadership development and enhancing customer service through developing employee engagement.

Through all of her career she has had an interest in people and the psychology around why they do what they do and how you can better gain self awareness and sustained personal growth. This has lead her to train in a number of areas: Positive Psychology, Executive Coaching, NLP, Time to Think Techniques to name a few.

She has consistently come across very capable people who have at times struggled with aspects of their life and noticed that personal resilience is often the key to positively dealing with these set backs. She has through her personal experience, working with others and extensive reading around resilience, developed her thinking around the subject and what the key elements to it are and how you can work to develop your resilience. She shares her thoughts through seven inspirational stories from ordinary women she has met along side giving you thoughts ideas and strategies to develop your resilience.

Dedicated to

My Loving husband Mark and
my two amazing children
Emily and William

Contents

About the Author

Introduction   xi
The Tree of Resilience   xiii
The Acorns of Resilient Growth   xiv

Lauren's Story   1
Act As If   1
Key Areas of resilience that Lauren demonstrated   15
Strategies to develop resilience Lauren Style   17

Marie's Story   25
Knowing and Believing what you are Capable of   25
Key Areas of resilience that Marie demonstrated   33
Strategies to develop resilience Marie style   35

Jane's Story   42
The Power of Self Belief   42
Key areas of resilience that Jane demonstrated   55
Strategies to develop resilience Jane style   57

Sarah's Story   60
Rediscovering Who I Am   60
Key areas of resilience Sarah demonstrated   71
Strategies to develop resilience Sarah Style   72

Clare's Story   77

Dealing with Constant Knock Backs   77

Key areas of resilience Clare demonstrated   97

Strategies to develop resilience Clare style   98

Sarah's Cressesll's Story   104

The Power of Passion and Goal Setting   104

Key areas of resilience Sarah demonstrated   118

Strategies to develop resilience Sarah style   119

Julie's Story   123

Realising It Wasn't My Fault   123

Key areas of resilience Julie demonstrated   143

Strategies to develop resilience Julie style   145

The Acorns of Resilient Growth a reminder   157

Summary   162

Introduction

I woke up this morning with a sense of energy and clear direction; I believe this has come about from a number of activities over the previous months.

Where did it start? It started with a dream, developed through the Disney Technique which I will share with you later in the book. The dream was unclear but I had a strong image of me, in front of others, in my bright pink dress – a dress that had been bought but never worn at this stage. And there's another story: what was holding me back from wearing such a stunning dress and what would finally lead me to wear it?

In the dream I was talking to lots of people but what was I saying? I do not know. There was writing, and what did that mean? Again I do not know but for some reason I felt absolutely sure this was part of the future – my future. I also saw an image of me 'high diving', taking part in a show with others and, amazingly, doing a dive – one that was full of twists and turns before I entered the water with the perfect entry.

What did this all mean? Again I do not know. But I was sure it didn't mean I was going to become a 'Tom Daley'.

What I am getting a clear sense of though, is that I have more to offer to others and that I am capable of much more, if only I can find the direction in which to travel and if only I can be brave enough – brave enough to put my head up above the parapet and fulfil this dream, my dream.

All of this was in my subconscious, obviously working its magic, as it often does. We don't really understand or use the power of our unconscious mind but maybe we should.

And what else has led me to this morning and having the compelling urge to write this book?

Well I recently went to see a medium (Joanne Gregory) and had my 'cards' read. Through her amazing skill, she sowed the seeds of what is possible, and what might occur if I am ready to take the opportunities which present themselves to me. She unlocked a part of my psyche which makes me so very hard on myself. Many of us are hard on ourselves and how limiting is that for us emotionally and professionally?

The last thing which brought all of this together, brought the clear picture and desire to write this book, yesterday I allowed myself some time out from my normal world to have lunch with a friend. This friend enabled me to escape, be totally in the moment and happy. I was already happy but somehow this friend had the ability to free me of all that was whizzing in my head, the stuff I 'should' be doing, the stuff I 'needed' to do, the list of chores and jobs – all the things that bog us down, disempower us and keep us from what we are really capable of.

I have been reading a book recently about developing your creative dream and one of the aspects that the author mentions is to take time out from your busy life, allow yourself to rest, and then the dreams will flow.

A safe, carefree environment, a special friend and suddenly everything – anything – seems possible.

This morning, during those great early waking moments – a time which is excellent for clarity of thought – my mind was full of pictures and messages, multiplying by the minute as I lay there. I was talking to myself about what my book might be called, and why. What it would be about and who would be included in it; how so many normal women travel through their life but have inspirational stories to tell. That it would have strategies and techniques to help other women going through difficulties so they could help themselves and be reassured by the stories they have read.

Throughout my life I have been fortunate to meet lots of great individuals and many of the women I have met seem to have achieved more than they thought was possible, that life at certain times for them was difficult and challenging. These women are like you and I, ordinary everyday women.

I am going to share with you some of their stories which I hope will relate to your own personal situation. I am going to share some great tips and techniques to develop your resilience. All of the tips and techniques are tried and tested, if not by me, then by others I have coached or who have been kind enough to share their wonderful experiences with me from various stages of their full and interesting lives.

As I share these great experiences and techniques with you, I am sure that life will appear easier than you think. Often it's just about trusting that inner voice, having a little faith to step forward; then once you start to move you'll be surprised at how life can send you things to help you on your journey to achieve and do what you want. You just have to be open to them.

The Tree of Resilience

Having worked with people for a number of years and read around the subject of resilience, positive psychology, emotional intelliegence and general well-being, in this book I share my thinking in connection with what the key elements to resilience are and how you can develop them, so when you come across life's difficulties you have the skills to be able to deal with them.

The tree resembles the essence of nature for me and has an amazing ability to adapt and grow as the world changes around it, which is a great metaphor for developing yourself for life's difficulties. Each situation is a learning opportunity though at the time this is exceptionally difficult to believe: but it's true, if we learn from our experiences and develop ourselves we, like nature, adapt and grow.

On my Resilience Tree there are eight acorns that, if nurtured and developed, will grow and prosper. These acorns hold the key to developing your resilience. Within the book, after each person's story, I reflect on what elements of resilience did they learn, develop and grow and I share ideas on how you can develop yours.

The Acorns of Resilient Growth

 Self-efficacy – generally the confidence and belief in one's ability.

From the work Bandura, a leading American psychologist recognised for contributions to many fields of psychology and the originator of the theory of self efficacy. When researching self-efficacy he noticed how people's beliefs impacted on their levels of motivation and perseverance when they overcame obstacles. He recognised that most success requires persistent efforts, so low self-efficacy becomes a self-limiting process. In a nutshell, if you have a healthy belief in your own ability and a confidence around what you can do then this will take you a long way in achieving success despite the difficulties you face. Within Marie's story we expand on this further.

 Optimism – the extent to which you believe you will experience good outcomes. A tendancy to expect the best possible outcome.

The pessimist sees the difficulty in every opportunity: an optimist sees the opportunity in every difficulty. – Winston Churchill.

This quote captures it all for me. Developing an optimistic approach to life in general will have a significant impact on your well-being and outlook, as well as your overall resilience.

Another way of putting it – hopefulness and confidence about the future or the success of something.

Humour – the ability to see the humorous side and use humour to alleviate situations.

The definition of a sense of humour is: 'The ability to perceive, relate and experience a given situation in a funny and amusing way'. Having an ability to laugh at oneself and make others laugh helps alleviate how you and others may feel. Adding humour will help you through challenges; seeing the funny side or just making sure you make time to have fun helps regenerate us, boost our energy and often helps put a different perspective on the situation.

Emotional self-control – the ability to understand and control your impulsive emotions and feelings.

People who tend to perform well in this area display an element of grace and calmness under pressure. They think clearly and stay focused, often having high stamina as energy is not wasted on high emotions. Remaining cool when under pressure and not letting things escalate when provoked or confronted is a fantastic skill to have. It's not a case of whether you are or you aren't such a person, this can be developed and when you are more in control of how you choose to react, it has a massive impact on you and others, especially in how you deal with difficulties and challenges.

 Purpose and clarity of direction – the extent to which you are clear on where you are heading, and have a sense of purpose around the things that you do.

The ability to set and commit to goals and achieve them is vital. Having a clear understanding of what's important to you, your personal values, and having a bigger connection to the things that you do enables you to move beyond the current issues and challenges. Knowing why and what is important helps you see beyond the immediate.

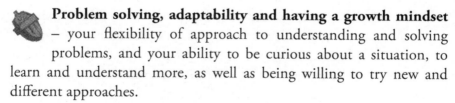 **Problem solving, adaptability and having a growth mindset** – your flexibility of approach to understanding and solving problems, and your ability to be curious about a situation, to learn and understand more, as well as being willing to try new and different approaches.

It's important to have a learning approach to your life rather than a fixed mindset which closes down your thinking that things can change and be different. Your ability to identify and remove internal and external blocks to change is crucial as well as your willingness to adapt and change your behaviour and responses to the changing situations. All these aspects give you more flexibility and skills in how you work through difficulties.

Perspective – your ability to see things from a different angle, or another's viewpoint, opening up your view of the situation which helps you see things as they really are, not as they seem.

Our personal perspective is extremely powerful in getting us to believe that viewpoint. When we learn how to stand back or hover above the situation it opens up our perspective on the situation, we see more and it is often not as we first thought, giving us a more realistic interpretation of the situation. Once we have this we are better equipped to understand what to do.

 Support – this is in three facets, your ability to ask others for help, your ability to support yourself and be kind to yourself and supporting others.

At times you can be your biggest supporter or worst enemy and learning how to support yourself through managing your negative self-talk, your health and fitness, is a key place to start. Also knowing what help you need from others and asking for it enables you to increase your personal resources. Helping others gives you a sense of meaning and feel good factor, which helps build your resilience.

As well as the eight acorns that you can grow and develop for yourself it's important for me to add also the importance of general health. Being fit and healthy increases your levels of resilience, improves your energy, and exercise releases endorphins, neurotransmitters, produced as a response to certain stimuli especially stress, fear and pain and interacts mainly as a receptor in cells in regions of the brain responsible for blocking pain and controlling emotion. Exercise is a natural way of releasing more of these in to your body. In connection with general health and well being I have found there are four key areas to consider:

- What you eat
- How you sleep and rest
- How often you exercise
- What time you spend in the fresh air

Physical exercise boosts your mood and releases endorphins; it increases self-confidence and sense of control. It distracts from negative thoughts and emotions and helps alleviate stress and anxiety. A regular exercise routine – it doesn't have to be hard core, just time to get yourself doing something – is a requirement to support your resilience. Find a friend to do it with; making a commitment to another person leads to greater consistency of exercise. Find something you enjoy; don't make it a burden, if you don't like the gym then don't go, find something more enjoyable.

Personally I'm into mountain biking, it gets me into the fresh air, sometimes I do it with a friend or my family, other times I quite like the time for me. I feel great, refreshed and invigorated when I return – not saying I don't ache the next day sometimes, but it's a good ache.

Fresh air - yes, your gran and your mother, were right. There is research that shows that just 10-15 minutes per day in green space, outside connecting with trees, grass and nature, will have a positive impact on how you feel. Which in turn ensures that you are more likely to be upbeat and positive, thus more creative and have a balanced perspective on things. Thus developing your resilience. So get out for a walk, a cycle, a run – yes, even in the rain. Just go and sit in your garden or the park, soak in the nature around you.

What you eat, is all about the things we know and often forget. I had a client recently that was tired, feeling down and had found herself reaching for the biscuits and eating high sugar and fatty foods to comfort her. Luckily she listened to her body which was craving for more nutritious and healthy food, she got back into a routine of eating fruit and vegetables and soon found she was feeling like she had more energy for longer. I'm not suggesting those treats aren't allowed it's more about balance and making sure that your diet provides the necessary vitamins and nutrients to help you with your energy levels. The other key aspect here is regular healthy meals, don't be tempted due to time pressures or the feeling of 'I cant be bothered' to drop a meal. Your body requires regular nourishment to function at its optimum.

You will find more on each of these 'acrons' at the end of each chapter and how you can develop them. The seven women's stories, including my own are there to help create a connection and understanding that we all have difficulties and challenges.

I hope you find a connection from these seven women's stories that helps inspire you and shows that it is possible to change your situation –that you can do something about it despite at times not thinking you can and not knowing what to do. The tips and exercises are there for you to dip into to develop your resilience, helping to strengthen what you already have and help you with life's difficulties, whatever the size.

I would love to hear your thoughts on what I have written and I hope, as I had intended, it helps.

> *The strongest oak of the forest is not the one protected from the storm and hidden from the sun. It's the one that stands in the open where it is compelled to struggle for existence against the winds and the rains and the scorching sun.* – Napoleon Hill. Author – Think and Grow Rich

Chapter 1

LAUREN'S STORY – "ACT AS IF"

Today is New Year's Eve and I'm suffering from a rather nasty batch of flu; doing exactly what the doctor suggested, I have been taking it easy this morning lying in bed. Often when I do this I find my brain works overtime. I have been thinking about the fact that I decided to write a book. This book. Not sure why but I only told two people – my coach and a friend; the friend would probably tell you it's all about whether I believe in myself enough to tell the world, the threat of being laughed at. It could be that or it could be that I don't yet feel like a writer.

So what is a writer like? Well I have tried the whole JK Rowling approach, dropped my son at school and then going to a coffee shop. I sat with my cappuccino and journal and wrote whatever came into my head about the amazing women I have come across. This approach worked for a while then work got busy and it was more a case of grabbing a quick takeaway coffee. So the JK Rowling approach hasn't consistently worked for me.

This morning while lazing in bed, the whole subject of 'Act as if' floated into my head. It made me think about me as a writer and I asked myself again: What is a writer? A friend of mine told me that Jeffrey Archer, when he works on his novels, he is extremely disciplined; he writes for so many hours, then has a break, and then starts again, and so on, pretty much doing this for the full day. I can't remember the exact detail but my friend said she understood it didn't take him long at all to write the blockbuster *Kane and Abel* with this technique. Mind you, she also dropped in that he was somewhere warm and sunny, in one of his houses, no doubt with no domestic chores or other duties that had to be fitted in. Might make a good excuse to say to the hubby, 'I'm off to Tenerife for a week or so to write a book. Can you sort the children out?' Then again . . .

So this morning I've drawn a different picture: believing that writers are some how free flowing with their creativity, I feel the ideas will develop when they are ready and then I'll be inspired to write. This morning I felt the urge to get up and write, so I got myself some toast and lashings of butter and strawberry jam – writers need to feed their imagination and, I thought, we aren't in the New Year yet so the diet doesn't have to kick in. A cup of tea and here I am sitting at the laptop. Could really do with a gadget that takes the ideas from my head as I get them and turns them into the written word –those great ideas I seemed to have earlier have become a bit jumbled or lost again in the brain.

So 'Act as if' – some of my coaching colleagues don't agree with this technique, however personally I have found that it has a great place to start in really helping somebody work towards where they want to be. To illustrate my thinking I'd like to introduce you to an amazing woman, Lauren.

When I first met Lauren she had recently become a Director of an American company based in the UK. She wanted a coach to help her work on a number of self-development aspects to enhance her performance. This was her first appointment as a Director and she had also previously changed companies. She had already conducted a 360 degree feedback and was clear on what she wanted to work on for her personal development. Lauren is exceptionally driven to achieve and be successful; as you would expect, she was clear on what she was looking for from a coach and she knew what her weaker spots were.

In one of the early sessions, Lauren spoke about the fact that the role of Director still didn't seem to 'fit right' on her. It was like an ill-fitting jumper, one that scratches a little and feels uncomfortable. Through exploring this we discovered that she didn't believe she was a Director – the title belonged to somebody else, not her. Her confidence had been knocked in her previous company where she had found herself working in a department that was bullying in its nature, that really didn't care about the people, they just wanted results and weren't particularly bothered how they got them. Lauren had found the strength to find herself a better career fit, a company that appeared to value its people and one where she was valued for her contribution. This knock in confidence however was still lurking beneath the surface and was one of the reasons why the new title didn't fit. She hadn't been prepared for the new position as you might be if you get an internal promotion, and this was another factor that made it difficult for her to accept the title.

One of the things we did was to explore what successful Directors look like. Her description initially reflected men; their sleek suits, polished shoes, their crisp shirts. These Directors were well groomed, they moved with confidence, erect and purposeful, walked at a reasonable pace. She described how they sat in meetings, what they did in meetings, concentrating and interjecting just at the right moment with a pertinent point which would always be extremely insightful. 'They' weren't distracted with blackberries or missing the point of the meeting. They often controlled the direction in which the meeting was going, although in a way that people felt included. Lauren built a powerful picture describing what she felt was the image and behaviour of a successful Director.

So the 'Act as if' approach is all about doing exactly that. OK, you've built a great picture in your head, just copy it and pretend *you are* that successful person. Lauren worked on the look that she would create. The interesting thing was that in her wardrobe she had these 'kind of skirt suits', but since being in this position she hadn't worn them. She had accent scarves to add a bit of attention to the dark suits and make her own mark. She also had some 'power shoes'. (Personally I think shoes tell a great story about the person and are an easy way to add an element of personality within the often constrained worlds of formal organisations. I remember once having a conversation with a fellow board member about my shoes. I was dressed in a dark dress with a white shirt underneath it, so fairly conservative; my shoes however were my element of rebellion and fun – red patent leather with a wedge heel of leopard skin, gorgeous. Do I need to say any more?)

Lauren sat more erect as we were discussing what successful Directors do. When I asked her how she felt now she was sitting differently, she considered this and then reflected that she felt more able.

We planned together what the next few days would look like, what she would wear, how she would sit in meetings and walk down the corridor, to truly connect with what she had observed in others.

From the following day Lauren dressed differently and acted differently, preparing herself for the role of 'successful Director'.

This technique enables you to imagine a particular situation and clearly build the picture, or look at others who do this well and copy them. As I mentioned about the writers, what do they do? How have they achieved success in the world of writing a book?

There is a great little story that Lauren tells about herself after we had been working together for a while. She was going to a conference, in fact I think her area was hosting it, and she had an opportunity to launch herself in the international arena of her company. Because she had now become clear on what she should look like as a 'successful Director', she needed an exceptionally large suitcase to create this image and she became recognised at the conference as the person with the largest case. Because her self-confidence at this stage was so good, she was able to take these comments in her stride and make a joke about it. She got herself noticed for many reasons at that conference, her humour and professional image being just two of them. The others I will share with you later.

I have recently been to see an excellent production of the King and I with my daughter and Anna, the English nanny when she is afraid sings a great song "When ever I feel afraid". The words talk about her whistling a happy tune and holding her head up high, deceiving others of how she really feels. Play it for yourself and see how it makes you feel.

This really connects with the 'Act as if' approach – through adopting a persona, and characteristics of what you have imagined, you then build your own self-confidence and ability naturally. It's a great place to start.

Let's go back a little for me to explain a bit more about Lauren before I share with you the rest of her story.

Lauren is an attractive, smart, intelligent business woman who balances being a mother, wife and homemaker. Her role requires her to make European travel trips, which will increase as her responsibilities grow and change into a European rather than just a UK role.

She had arranged support in the home to help her with these challenges – a cleaner and, when I first started coaching her, a nanny to help take the children to and from school – although this proved a cause of stress and soon changed.

Despite Lauren being very focused about what she wanted to work on, which we will cover later, I kept hearing some unusual things that she said: 'Are they going to find out?'; 'Do I have the knowledge to pull this off?', all linked to how she described her role as Director. I felt that this was touching on the real issue so we explored her thoughts and beliefs about her position as a Director further.

We did an exercise that unlocked a limiting belief that she had: 'I'm not good enough to be a Director'. This in itself was quite emotional for Lauren. Coming face to face with what was lurking underneath and often pulling her back from achieving what she set out to do was immensely powerful. We also explored where it came from, how it had developed as a belief and what had fuelled it during her life to date. Being able to look back at these aspects with a greater understanding of its impact enabled Lauren to question this belief and make it a little wobbly.

We were then able to replace this 'limiting' belief with a new, more empowering and supportive belief. This sounds easy, but getting Lauren to be able to say this out loud, in a convincing and confident manner, was difficult. The old self-doubt kicked in and tried to pull her back down, making her question this new confident belief. Lauren *did* master it and as she started to believe it, you could see her whole persona change; she smiled and she sat confidently with her shoulders back and her head held high.

Her homework from the session was to continue to say her new belief out loud every morning and night until the new belief was firmly cemented into her being and she knew, without a shadow of a doubt, that it was true.

When she arrived for the next session I knew that the new belief was absolutely part of her; the way she looked and walked into the session confirmed to me that she was a 'great Director'.

To expand on this further we really worked on what a great Director does and how they behave. We had done the 'What do they look like?' and 'What do they wear?' and 'How do they walk and sit?' as I mentioned earlier. She had swapped the trousers to skirt suits and was looking like those crisp Directors she had previously described. What also made this even more powerful is that people noticed and commented on how she looked.

Receiving compliments is such a powerful and positive feeling that we often underestimate and dismiss, rather than accepting them gracefully and thanking the person for the compliment. If you allow yourself they make you feel great and really boost your self-confidence. I love receiving them; have to say though the best person I know who gives them to me is my son. He often notices when I look good and says, 'Mum you look nice today'. What a great skill. I hope he keeps it, as some lucky woman will really appreciate it when he's older.

Through this exploration of behaviours, Lauren surprised herself with what she discovered about herself. She recognised that a Director would confidently express an opinion in a meeting and not hold back. She realised that despite what the subject matter was and especially if it wasn't immediately the individual's responsibility, they would still be attentive and contribute on wider subjects about the business. When exploring this Lauren noticed that she didn't: she only really focused on her area and was so worried about being questioned that she didn't truly listen to her colleagues.

In certain sized meetings with certain people, peers and seniors, she was more reserved and didn't express her thoughts. She had the thoughts; they floated in her head but she was so tied up in the negative self-talk around this that the moment would pass and the thought gone.

Negative self-talk can be a real enemy; it takes over, convincing us that whatever it's saying is right – it is so persuasive.

We had also discovered through doing a psychometric profile on Lauren that she thought things through in absolute detail, considering all the pros and cons and aspects, requiring all the facts and information to take into consideration. These two aspects were getting in the way of her positively contributing in meetings.

Did she really need to check all that detail? What instinctively did she think? When she had those instinctive thoughts and she had listened to them and then checked herself with the detail, how often was she right? Surprisingly, most of the time; she knew her stuff and her instincts were often right but she had got used to the comfort blanket of checking the facts and figures before she passed a viewpoint. The comfort blanket has a purpose in life for a period of time, however, if we have them for too long they become a crutch, a false necessity that limits us really reaching our potential. It was time to lay aside the familiar and safe comfort blanket and start to act without it and really show herself what she was capable of.

We worked on a new self-talk that shut the other one up and allowed Lauren to voice what she was thinking. Yes, it was about taking risks, but we worked on when and what would be an acceptable first risk to try this out, and build on her successes. Lauren was brave and determined to succeed in this role, which enabled her to move forward on this with determination; she was prepared to just give it a go and see what happened.

Lauren now contributes in meetings no matter who is present. Yes, she still prepares and gains information that will potentially support the discussion. However, if she hasn't got it but has a thought, or viewpoint, she now expresses it confidently, just as that 'great Director' she described in the earlier sessions would.

The other aspect that came up was about taking part in meetings even if it wasn't her area of expertise, which linked to being a role model. What do employees expect of Directors in meetings? What we identified was that there was a bit of a culture in some meetings of senior people dealing with their blackberries rather than listening respectfully to the content. Often the reason was that the content wasn't great. What we discovered through this conversation was that it was often less senior people who didn't deliver the required information in the right way or delivered the wrong content. But nobody helped them address and change this, nobody gave them feedback – what happened was that the senior members got distracted and busied themselves with other things while being half present in the meeting.

Once we had created this picture of what occurred, Lauren didn't like this aspect about herself and felt that as a Director she had a responsibility to change what was happening, rather than joining in and reinforcing this culture. Was this an easy option? No – but her view was that if a Director didn't feel certain behaviours were right then they should identify the reasons behind them and make changes. Absolutely, I say. She became the unofficial chair in many meetings; as the designated chair was often not very effective, she moved things on, assisted the chair to get agendas out in advance, ensured the correct people were invited to the right meetings and that expectations were made clear about the input required. This was done in a very supportive and developmental manner whilst not ducking the issue of giving feedback to both her peers and line manager about how the meetings could be improved.

Previously she would have moaned about what a waste of time the meeting was, how badly managed it was, that the right people weren't there, etc, etc. She moved to being a person that looked for solutions on how to make improvements and identified what needed altering, influencing others to change with her. She changed her approach from a negative one, 'let me join in with the behaviour that happens', into a positive 'we can change this and I can impact on those changes'.

Peers and senior people started to notice how she was making a difference in the meetings she was at, and that those meetings were now often more productive than they had been.

This more positive approach she started to develop stretched to other areas of her work with her looking for solutions and outcomes rather than problems. I don't know about you but I much prefer to be with positive people, those people who feel that things are possible even if they haven't found the solution yet, but know they will.

People within the organisation started to seek her out and valued her viewpoints on different aspects.

There was one issue that kept reoccurring within the sessions that we had and that was Lauren's concern about how she, at times, with certain people, felt she needed to be right. The impact of this was that she dug her heels in and forced her opinion on the other person, not listening or trying to influence, just being fairly aggressive about getting her point across. Rather than her normal good natured personality, it was as though the wicked witch had got hold of her personality and was controlling her for a while as she didn't feel she could control her reactions.

Have you ever had that situation? You know that what you are doing is probably not the best way to get the result you want but you feel out of control and your reaction to a situation is automatic and responsive. Afterwards, when you think about it, you really wish you hadn't taken that approach. It's almost as if you were possessed by somebody else at the time.

Through really breaking the situation down we were able to identify what the trigger was with Lauren, what it was that seemed to tip her into this behaviour that she felt she couldn't control. It's important to understand the logic behind the illogical responses you often have to situations, really understanding the reasons why you behave in this way. We were also able to get her to notice what signals her body was giving her. The body is a fantastic early warning system in aspects like this, it speaks to you and gives you messages; the skill is listening to it – tuning into what the messages mean. Lauren was able to work out what the indicators were and know that if she felt these sensations then her likely automatic reaction would be the behaviours she didn't want to continue. Once she was aware of that she was able to use this to 'break state', as we say. She took heed of the early warning system and chose to do something else to take her out of what was about to lead her down the path of losing control. This became a technique that she used to have control over her reactions rather than feeling controlled by another force.

There was one particular individual that she tended to push her view onto, and really often their conversations ended in a conflict situation, with both parties feeling a lose-lose situation. Recognising that this was not helpful, her logical brain was telling her to do something about it, her emotional brain was pulling against this and resisting.

We opened this up really gently by getting Lauren to see the situation from a different perspective, really putting herself in the other person's shoes, as well as getting her to take an objective non-emotional view of both herself and the other person. We used an exercise called Perceptual Positions, which really gets you sitting in the other person's shoes and taking on their persona. We often say, 'sit in the other person's shoes' but don't often capture the potential great insights from really doing it.

With the insights from this, Lauren was able to take a whole different approach to future conversations with this individual; understanding better where he was coming from and what he might be thinking and feeling really helped her change her approach. She started to listen to what he was saying and explore his points and genuinely ask questions of interest, really understanding his perspective and point of view. Only after she had this understanding did she then discuss her thinking. What she also noticed was that because she had genuinely listened to the other person, he was more prepared to listen to her point of view – rather than the previous situation with each of them talking aggressively, both at the same time, and neither one of them listening.

As Stephen Covey explains in his book *The 7 Habits of Highly Effective People* – 'Seek first to understand and then be understood'.

This new approach not only improved the results Lauren achieved with this particular individual and his area but also enhanced her conversations and discussions with others – really considering their view and perspective in the situation rather than being so concerned about getting her point across. Her initial aim was to understand the other person's point of view and then consider how that linked to her point of view. What she found was that conversations became easier and less of a battle, she enjoyed them more, and it took less energy to get her points listened to and heard.

This led us on to looking at her influencing ability even further, especially at influencing upwards. Having worked in a number of organisations before she came to this role, she possessed an exceptional amount of experience and knowledge and ideas of different approaches that could be taken by the business. But if you can't get the right people to hear and act upon them, you often feel frustrated and rejected, potentially tipping you into a false assessment of the organisation and your role in it, thinking 'What's the point, I know how to solve that problem but nobody listens to me'.

Having the ideas is one thing; the real skill that is needed alongside this is your ability to influence others. Really honing this skill, especially at senior levels within an organisation, is a necessity for career and business progression.

Initially with Lauren it was about identifying her successful results in influencing, as well as looking at when things didn't go so well for her. Being more conscious of this and starting to reflect on what went well and what didn't go well and noting these down, helped unpick both how she was having successes and where things weren't going as well as she would have liked. Honing in on the aspects that worked for her and identifying where her blockers were, led to identifying the pattern that worked best for influencing and how to repeat it more often.

I had left Lauren working on these aspects when our time came to an end; she was entering a new senior development programme as she had been recognised by her company as somebody that they wanted to support for continued progression. Along with this programme she got the opportunity to have a different coach. I have no doubt that Lauren is continuing to progress and enhance her skills further. As our coaching came to an end she was entering into another new role as the company reorganised again. To help her visualise and start to get to grips with this new role we spent time working on what it would be like.

We did an exercise called Neurological Levels – Dilts. What this did was explore the role at a number of different levels to really make it come to life for her, making the picture clearer in her head, enabling her to identify the key priorities and skills she would need. What behaviours

11

will she engage in, what will she be doing? What capabilities will she be using, what skills will she be practising? What are her values and beliefs in this new role, what is important to her about it? Who is she in this area of her life, what's her identity. Exploring all the levels really opens up the thinking and subconscious to broader aspects than you would normally consider. This enabled Lauren to fully reflect on what the role was all about and better plan for entering that world.

Alongside this career-related development, we did work on the other sides of her life. I'm a believer in getting the key aspects in balance. Being all work and no play, so to speak, really doesn't make for a happy, rounded and fulfilled individual and potentially negatively impacts on your resilience levels.

Early on Lauren spoke about being exhausted and tired all the time, often getting home and collapsing and really not being her best self with the family. Previously she had had a reasonable exercise routine, however since joining this company with the challenges of the new role, and the travel, along with all the other aspects, exercise was a thing of the past.

After exploring how being fit made her feel, she wanted to add this back into her weekly routine. Initially she didn't travel too much abroad so she took to running during her lunch break, not far and not too strenuously, but getting out in the fresh air and taking time out to reinvest in her health. It became an appointment in her electronic diary so others couldn't book her during these times. She also added exercise in at home and where possible combined it with activities with her children; it soon became a normal function of her week.

She felt more energetic and alive and just generally better as a result. Exercise releases endorphins which are the natural 'feel good' drug within ourselves, so as well as getting our bodies in a healthier state for long term health, it also makes you feel great. Who wouldn't want to feel great? But there are lots of reasons why we put it off. With Lauren we were able to tap into the motivation of how it would make her feel better. She is a person who asks 'How can things improve, what can be more pleasurable?' If you understand your personal motivators you can tap into these to help you take action. Are you a person who moves towards pleasure like Lauren, or do you move away from pain?

Lauren's exercise routine got a little knocked off course when her travel schedule became a little crazy and also she was still not feeling quite right health-wise, which did actually end up in an operation to rectify.

This is also an interesting insight to Lauren. If you had told her when I first started working with her that she was going to have to take two or three months off work, this would potentially have caused much stress and concern. However, when this arose she was in a much better place, more confident about herself and her team; it was now less about having all the control and more about effectively managing her team. This gave her the confidence that she could take the time out to manage her health issues, and build back slowly working from home to ensure she was in full health before returning to her extensive European travel plans.

Lauren came across many obstacles along her road to success. She demonstrated determination to find the answers and a better way of doing things. She worked hard at her personal development which enabled her to grow as an individual, positively impacting on all aspects of her life. She could have given up and thought that changing herself was too difficult but she didn't and as she saw the results this propelled her forward even more.

Lauren found more energy to have a more rewarding time with her children, rather than flaking out on the sofa at night.

I mentioned earlier that her nanny at times caused her emotional angst. She wasn't quite doing things as Lauren wanted. A specific part of Lauren's personality was getting in the way again. Rather than appreciating what the nanny did, Lauren focused on picking faults with the nanny in her head. Lauren felt she needed to discuss matters with the nanny, but felt at the time so reliant on her support that she didn't want to cause friction so avoided the conversations. Tension then just built up with Lauren, draining her energy. We discussed her concerns and how real they might be and what was the most likely reaction of the nanny. We worked out a number of strategies for delivering the feedback, giving her confidence around how to handle it. Lauren delivered the feedback and all was OK. Through understanding this and the way to truly understand another person's perspective she developed a more appreciative relationship with her mum as well. You can only really change yourself or how you respond to situations you can't change the other person, so getting a different perspective on her relationship with her mum helped Lauren. This understanding enabled Lauren to be more patient and handle her mum differently which really enhanced their relationship.

Before we leave Lauren, it's important that I share with you one of her great successes. I mentioned it briefly before, the international conference. Lauren and her department were given the opportunity to host and headline a major conference where there would be major company Directors as well as other country Directors such as herself. This filled Lauren with real mixed emotions. Her logical self knew this was a great opportunity to show others what she had been leading her team in working on and the positive business impacts she was having. But her emotional, wobbly-confidence self didn't see it like that at all. She had previously, as I've mentioned, been avoiding speaking up in European meetings, and especially had avoided more senior people. The fact that she would be on the stage in front of a large audience with all eyes and ears on her really made her question her ability again. She was not only having to ensure she was going to be great but she was leading her team through this too. Lauren being Lauren had all the data and facts; there was never an issue about the content of her presentation or in how she would put it across, ensuring a good balance between information and data as well as the content on the slides. She had great strength in getting the pitch right for her audience whilst ensuring it was backed up with data.

For Lauren it was about whether she would meet the expectations of what others were looking for, whether she had what it took to stand up there and present herself in a professional capable way. Despite all the work we had been doing this seemed to knock her back and reconnected with how she was feeling when I first started working with her. We worked on a number of things to rebuild her confidence and connect with where she was in reality, not the picture she was painting in her head. We ran through things in detail, imagining and painting pictures for her brain to connect with. These replaced the negative ones that had been whizzing round initially. We had a quick session on her way to the conference on the phone in the airport to keep that positive focus and picture. I sent a brief email before she was due on stage to remind her of her talent and capabilities. She went out with her head held high with that Director walk and her new suit and shoes, no doubt looking a million dollars. She breathed slowly and purposefully and presented her message flawlessly.

What was great about this was that for Lauren this didn't end there, she didn't fall in a heap and think 'Great, done, I can find a corner and hide'. We had talked about how she needed to seize the opportunity this event would give her and seek out senior people and make conversation with them, having planned in advance what they might be interested in so she could ensure it was a good conversation and that she was able to talk on a diverse number of topics around the business.

This had been a big occasion for Lauren and she had planned for it and seized it, really making it hers. It created an opportunity for her to show herself what she was capable of as well as other senior people in the organisation that she hadn't met before. It really propelled her forward.

Lauren found through her personal development, more balance, more energy and more career success. None of this would have been possible if she hadn't been determined to develop and grow personally. She had to really work on herself to achieve more of the whole of her life that she wanted. Her resilience through this period is demonstrated in many aspects. Others may say, why change, why put yourself through the difficulty of personal development? Lauren did and benefited from this in many ways.

Key areas of resilience that Lauren demonstrated
Self-efficacy

In connection with her position as a Director, Lauren didn't believe that this role 'fitted'. Her confidence around her ability to do this position had been shaken through previous experiences. So this was a key area of focus to work on which once enhanced had massive benefits and stimulated more positive change and development.

Problem solving, Adaptability and having a growth mindset

Lauren worked on understanding what her personal blockers were which enabled her to find the right solutions to move forward. With understanding you can ensure you find the right way forward. Having a growth mindset gave her an outlook that things could change and be different.

Perspective

Once Lauren began to see things from others' perspective, understanding how they saw things, how they felt, she was able to take a different approach with different relationships which enhanced them and the conflict disappeared.

Support

Lauren recognised she wanted to develop herself in her role as Director. She was clear on what she thought she needed to do but wasn't sure how, so she hired a professional coach to support her through her personal development.

She also had other professional and family support, which enabled her to do the role as well as being a mum and homemaker.

Reminders for me through writing this chapter

Often what we believe to be the issue isn't it at all. Lauren had initially diagnosed from her 360 the areas she felt she needed to work on. Once we started to work together it became clear that these specifics weren't the real issue – rather it was around her belief as to whether she thought she was a Director or not.

The other reminder is that self-development takes time and effort. Lauren persisted in seeking new and improved ways to behave to enhance her performance. At times this was difficult, new things are difficult to learn, especially when we are in the consciously incompetent stage and we are trying new techniques. As we become consciously competent it is still hard and takes considerable energy and effort. We benefit hugely if we persevere as we become unconsciously competent, we no longer have to think about it, it has become embedded in what we do, automatic. It's a bit like when you learn to drive, learning takes effort and energy and practice. Once we become a competent driver we do lots of things automatically and it seems to be so much easier.

Strategies to develop resilience Lauren-style

Self-efficacy

'Act as if' enables you to imagine a particular situation and clearly build a picture of what it will be like, or to copy what others do who are good at that particular skill or whatever you are striving to achieve.

Tips for helping you do this:

Be clear on what you want to be like, describe it fully, explore what it means, notice what that feels like as you describe it.

- Identify who you know who is like that.
- Look at famous people who are like that.
- What exactly do they do to be like that?
- What's their physical presence like?
- How do they dress?
- What do they sound like?
- How do they behave?
- What do they feel like in those situations?

Identifying these aspects gives you something to copy – 'Act as if' – which then, over time, leads to you being like that naturally, in your own way.

Limiting beliefs and affirmations

To identify what any limiting beliefs may be, ask yourself or maybe get a trusted friend to ask you:

- What stops you from .... ?
- Where do you hold yourself back?
- Which of my abilities should I be making the most of?
- What is my very first thought before I stop myself doing .... ?
- Where has this cropped up before? Where did it come from?
- Why do you think you can't? What makes you think that?

Once you have identified the limiting belief, here are a few more questions to help shift, remove or replace it:

- What does that belief cost you?
- What's the long-term cost if you don't let go?
- What would happen if you didn't let go of this?
- What would you like to believe instead?

Explore that new belief, imagine what it would be like if you adopted it; another way is to reframe your beliefs:

- Change the words subtly.
- Change the timeframe, the quicker you do this the easier it will seem.
- Find a counter-example; has there ever been a time when it has been easy?
- Challenge yourself for evidence; how do you know that?
- Appeal to the positive intention behind the belief. Often limiting beliefs are there to protect us, guide us, but we don't look at them in this way, as they tend to stop us from moving forward to where we want to be.

Once you have identified your limiting belief, you want to be able to find one to replace it that is more supportive:

- What do you want instead of the old belief?
- What will this new belief do for you?
- Always state it in the following way: 'I am'. State it in a positive way, what you will do, think, feel, say – as in Lauren's case, 'I am a great Director'.
- Write the belief out.
- Say it out loud to others.
- Place it where you will see it often.
- If you are a visual person, what image connects with this for you? Place a picture where you will see it often, such as a screen saver on your phone or PC.
- If you are a kinaesthetic person, what objective does it connect with. I had one client who was embedding his new belief of 'I am focused' and he carried in his briefcase a pair of binoculars, getting them out and placing them on his desk when he wanted to be focused.

Problem solving, adaptability and growth mindset

One of the techniques that Lauren used that wasn't in her story was the use of reflective practice. We tend not to take time to consider aspects that have just happened and therefore don't truly understand what and why things have happened – thus missing a huge learning opportunity. I give all my coaching clients a journal to capture their thoughts in and really encourage them to engage in reflective practice to enhance their personal development.

Developing reflective learning

Reflective learning is about exploring your experiences to understand how you learn so that you can improve your performance. As you develop your skills as a reflective learner you will become more self-aware and self-critical; be honest about yourself, and open to criticism and feedback; be more objective in weighing up evidence; be curious to discover other approaches and more motivated to improve your performance.

Reflective learning happens when you consciously think about and analyse what you do or have done, and we all do this to some degree. A structured approach helps you to reflect on your learning and to understand your own learning processes.

Getting started

Keep learning logs or journals. Writing reflectively can seem threatening to some and you may be turned off by the idea before you start. Begin slowly and take small steps to make reflective learning a habit.

An easy way to start is to structure the log by using set questions:

Description	What happened?
Feelings	What were you thinking and feeling?
	What was your personal behaviour?
	Did you have any concerns?
Evaluation	What was good and bad?
	Identify strengths and weaknesses.
Analysis	What did you make of the situation?
Conclusion	What else could you have done?
	List actions that enhanced or hindered the situation.
Action Plan	If it happened again, what would you do? What would you change?

Other approaches include:

Write from different perspectives – Describe your experience of an event in the third person to see a different viewpoint to the problem.

Unsent letter – Write the experience as an honest open letter to someone. Keep it in the learning journal.

Reflection on a book – Keep comments on what you are reading.

Learning partners/Critical friends – Get someone to help you compare and criticise the experience/approach, exchange ideas.

Describe the process of solving problems – Useful if you have a structured/staged problem-solving process.

Focus on past experience – Look for links with different experiences to get a new outlook or develop a more imaginative approach.

Lists – Write lists to generate ideas: 'What am I good at?', 'Things I could change'.

Stepping stones – For specific experiences list in chronological order what you remember about the 'event'.

At least every three weeks look over your log and reflect on the learning processes you have gone through.

- Did something go well? Then what did I learn from it? How can I build on it?
- Did something go badly? Then exactly what went wrong? How can I fix it, overcome difficulties, and improve upon it?
- Have my ideas changed? If so, why?

Perspective

The most powerful exercise I did with Lauren was a Neuro-Linguistic Programming (NLP) Exercise called Perceptual Positions. This can be done alone but is more powerful when someone else asks you the questions and directs you.

Perceptual positions

Perceptual positions is all about seeing things truly from another's perspective. It also helps you to look at a situation from the objective neutral position. These new insights help you view your reactions and feelings differently, leading to new behaviours around this situation going forward.

How does it work?

It is often useful to arrange three chairs in a triangle, all facing each other. You can then move to a different chair as you adopt a different person's position.

Position 1 – You – Chair 1

Take yourself back to the situation that has occurred, re-engage with the feelings you had, what was going on; really get back to the situation. If it helps, close your eyes to see yourself there again.

- How are you feeling?
- What is your behaviour?
- What do you believe about this situation?
- What's important to you?
- What is there for you to learn?
- How has your perception changed?

As you get up to move chair, shake off physically all those feelings and thoughts and leave them on the chair.

Position 2 – the 2nd Person – Chair 2

As you sit down, facing chair 1, adopt their posture, how would they be sitting, what would they be looking like, what's their facial expression like? Really place yourself in their shoes as you sit in this chair. Again if it helps, close your eyes to image you being them. For this next step you are them.

- How are you feeling?
- What is your behaviour?
- What do you believe about the situation?
- What's important to you?
- What is there for you to learn?
- How has your perception changed?

Stand up and again shake off all those thoughts and feelings, leaving them on the chair. If it helps, look out of the window and notice what you see, so you really disengage with that person.

Position 3 – Observer Position – Chair 3

Imagine as you sit down, looking at the other two individuals, that you are in the fly on the wall position: looking down and observing the reaction between the two people, able to hear all that is being said and feeling all the emotions from both sides.

- How are they both feeling?
- How are they both behaving?
- What do they both believe about the situation?
- What is important to both of them?
- What is there for both of them to learn?

Stand up, shake off your thoughts and feelings and take yourself back to the first chair. Bring with you all the new learning, insights and perceptions.

- What have you learnt?
- How has your perception changed?

Support

Lauren got professional help to support her with her personal development through hiring a Coach. If you are in the position to do this then I would advise you to seek out a Professional Executive Coach who is fully trained, receives regular supervision; then meet them, talk to them, to ensure you feel you can work with them. Coaching is very intimate and you need to feel you can trust them, so you can open up and really explore your personal development aspects. Don't be afraid to check out their references, or testimonials.

There are other ways of getting support: find a friend or colleague and make a commitment to each other to support each other with your aspects. Set the boundaries and ensure you work at how you will give supportive challenge and are free from judgement.

Seek out a mentor. I have been approached by people I don't know about supporting them in a mentoring rather than coaching relationship; this is often more guiding as well as supportively challenging. Think about what you need, identify who has this skill/ability and approach them. Then make it happen; arrange the sessions plan for the meetings so you utilise their time effectively.

Having someone who is supportive around what you are wanting to do and encourages you to take those steps is exceptionally powerful. This encouragement helps you to move forward and often they celebrate your successes with you, inspiring you to do more.

Whatever is bringing you down, get rid of it. Because you'll find that when you're free . . . your true self comes out. – Tina Turner.

Chapter 2

MARIE'S STORY – "KNOWING AND BELIEVING WHAT YOU'RE CAPABLE OF"

I met Marie on my first weekend training to be a coach; I was sitting as you do, having a cup of coffee before the session started, at some hotel in Manchester. This funkily-dressed lady with short, dark, spiky hair, who I thought was probably in her early fifties but looking good, despite struggling with the swing doors with her crutches managed it with an accomplished approach which demonstrated she had been in this situation many times before. There was a real sense of determination coming from her, whilst her softness came through with a beautiful, genuine smile.

She made her way over to the table where I was sitting and I asked her if she'd like me to get her a drink. Graciously she accepted and we then talked through the whole story about what had brought her to train as a coach, how far she was along the training programme, etc.

We sat together during the day and did many exercises together and, as we did, more of her story unfolded. This intrigued me and gave me a sense of what an amazing woman she was – dealing with problems which would have knocked many of us into a world of self-pity. Marie is a fighter and determined that despite the blows she has had, it is worth living, and she will make the most of the life she has.

Once I had decided to write this book I knew Marie had to be in it; despite the fact that I hadn't seen her for over a year I got back in touch and we met for lunch. I told her what I was doing and that I would very much like to write about her story. Here it is:

At the age of one she was diagnosed with polio and meningitis; the doctors initially felt there was nothing significantly wrong with her but she was lucky enough to have a nurse who instinctively knew that this child was seriously ill and whisked her off to hospital.

In those days, with these types of illnesses, she was admitted to a specialist fever hospital. Imagine being one year old and having an extended stay in a hospital, not knowing what was going on, and then not being able to have any physical contact with the two people in her life with whom she felt safe, her parents. They weren't allowed to physically be with her. The doctors and nurses were the only physical contact she had over an extensive period – none of the normal parent/child touch and gentle reassurances in those important early years, no hugs and kisses or physical comfort and reassurance which help to develop who we are. Communication must have also been difficult in these circumstances with her mum and dad being the other side of a glass wall and she a one year old not having a great vocabulary.

Did this impact on her future life? Absolutely – both physically and mentally.

By the age of two Marie had developed a strong sense of self-reliance, independence and having a fighting spirit. She wasn't particularly comfortable with human contact and her relationship with men had suffered – she associated them with pain, having been in the situation for a year where all the doctors were male and tended to inflict pain on her. When she came out of hospital her relationship with her father was difficult. Her mum, as you can imagine, became very protective of her, making up for the lost connection and closeness.

These traits of self-reliance and independence stayed with Marie through her adult life and become her mechanism for succeeding, knowing that if she wanted something then it was down to her to get it.

Marie's sense of devilment and humour developed early. She tells a story about her mum taking her into school; she was being pushed in a normal chair that had wheels on it, so attracted uncomfortable attention from others and they didn't know how to respond to her. As a young child she was sensitive to the fact that adults didn't speak *to* her – they spoke to her mum *about* her, assuming that she wasn't aware of what was being said. Marie decided then that if she was going to be treated like an idiot, then she'd behave like one.

On one occasion when someone spoke to her mum about Marie, she decided to dribble out of the side of her mouth; they were ignoring the fact that she understood all that was being said –there was never an acknowledgement or discussion with her.

After the event her mum was mortified by Marie's behaviour and gave her a telling off. It really made me laugh because it showed Marie's true personality – fighting back and not being ignored – even from that early age. Marie learnt from that incident how others saw her physical disability and that she had something to show others she was more than her physical limitations . This sense of having to prove herself runs throughout her life.

At some stage she moved from the local school, where she didn't really develop many friendships, to a specialist school for children with physical disabilities. She was picked up every day in a taxi – having an element of independence in this new arrangement. The school had no aspirations for the children, they didn't do sciences, and there was a limited curriculum that didn't work toward any recognised attainments or qualifications.

Marie tells many stories about some of the antics she and her friends got up to whilst she was there – showing her great sense of fun and adventure.

When a new teacher arrived from 'normal' stream education other opportunities began to open up for the children. Woodwork and metalwork were introduced and these were liberating for children with physical difficulties. Although she does still get frustrated with the fact that she struggles to walk and needs the assistance of her crutches which limits what she can do and how fast she can do it, Marie adapted as she grew and developed – not knowing anything other than the physical abilities she had. One of the benefits of the new teacher coming was that he identified Marie's intelligence; despite her lack of formal qualifications he got her an assessment at the local college to be able to carry on her education doing Maths and English.

Talk about 'feel the fear and do it anyway', Marie up until then had been cosseted, being taxied to school and supported in her fairly safe environment. Attending college presented many challenges – particularly the physical aspects of getting to the college on the bus and a long walk from the bus stop. Her drive to be accepted, and not seen only for her limitations, made her get up early so she could travel to the college before anyone else arrived. She also left after everyone else – not wanting others to see her struggling. They then got to know Marie beyond her physical limitations.

College made Marie feel like everyone else; she had a new belief in herself from achieving the placement – she was able to believe, 'I'm not thick'.

Having to adapt to normal life was a challenge; her fighting spirit, and her drive to prove to herself she could do this, pushed her to work exceptionally hard and to maximise her opportunities.

Marie left college and got a job as a shorthand typist with a sense somewhere within her that there was still more she could achieve, but not consciously being aware of this. She often spoke to a particular young woman like herself travelling to work on the bus. On one particular day her friend told her that she was attending a teacher training course and Marie's internal voice said, 'Well I can do that if she can'. This voice gave her the push she needed to move to the next goal and achieve more.

Our internal voice can be a friend, as in this case with Marie, the question is do we allow ourselves the time to explore what it is trying to tell us and then take action?

Marie took action: whilst still working, she travelled on a part time basis from Sheffield to Huddersfield and obtained her certificate of teaching. Not easy on many fronts – juggling working and studying is enough of a challenge, never mind the travel difficulty. The result though, at the end of this, was that she got a full-time teaching position. Was this enough for Marie? Only for a while until she compared herself with others in the college; she recognised that the ones who got on had a degree. Yes – you guessed this is where she went next. This internal drive to prove to herself that she could do what others could do took her to university whilst doing five days work in four. At this stage she was married with a small child and just in case you don't think that's enough to balance, Marie was also doing up a house they had bought.

Life became very focused – work, university, the house and the family and they didn't socialise much over this period. Marie found the whole studying process quite boring and difficult but she pushed herself through it. She had to get this qualification – she had to be as good, if not better, than anybody else.

She was constantly proving to herself that her physical abilities were not going to limit her and what she was capable of. She also wanted to change others' perceptions of her – that she was more than the disability. The link back to her story as a child, when she discovered that others didn't know how to deal with her, incensed her and drove her to try physical things – showing herself and others what she was capable of.

Marie taught herself from a book to swim at the age of ten.

At 20 she went horse riding and did judo, just to show she could.

Where did the degree take her? This, packaged with her desire to achieve more, led her to apply for a senior lecturer's position. Up against 17 other candidates, her sense of self-worth was boosted again when she was the successful candidate and gained the position. This has become a personal milestone in her life – underpinning her sense of achievement, self-recognition and what she is capable of. Another milestone was when Marie applied for a teacher exchange programme which took her off to Arizona to teach Maths. Roger, her husband, gave up his job to go with her, and their son, who didn't have a job at the time, also joined them during the year she was out there.

This position created further challenges academically because she had to learn the subject *and* adapt it to the American audience. But she developed in personal ways she had not even considered would come from this opportunity.

She changed, from being rather house proud, to relaxing and learning to go with the flow; to enjoy the moment. Marie and her husband often had other exchange teachers to stay from elsewhere in America; she met a range of different types of people and was open to the experiences they brought – allowing them to see *her* rather than the house proud veneer she had found herself showing when people came to visit in England. She also found herself accepting help rather than fighting to prove she could do many physical things herself.

Marie's biggest personal development was that she overcame the apprehension of hugging others. The childhood wariness of physical contact was firmly removed. Although she was happy with close touch with her husband and son, with friends and strangers she had resisted. Being in a country that was often larger than life, the full-on-hug greeting took her through a difficult learning stage and she is now happy to hug others.

While she was there Marie and Roger took the opportunity to fully explore and absorb as many experiences as possible. They went white water rafting and totally enjoyed the thrill and experience of tumbling down those water rapids at speed. Marie continually embraced life and what it had to offer her through rich experiences, not letting her physical challenges limit her thinking of what she could do. Personally I would find it a challenge to go white water rafting despite having the desire to do it. Mind you my mother in her early sixties overcame her fear of not being able to swim very well, or go out of her depth in water, and went white water rafting. Food for thought for me.

The experiences she put herself through, the openness to fully absorb the surroundings and the people she was with, provided a truly transformational experience for Marie. This resulted in her coming back home feeling that she could do anything. She had pushed herself into difficult, but growing, situations, she had opened herself up to let others see her as she truly was, rather than trying to hide or compensate for the physical disabilities she had. The 'whole' Marie emerged and blossomed.

As is often the case, when Marie returned home a different person from whom she had been, her current employment and position was no longer a place that totally fulfilled her. She wanted something different; the frustrations and bureaucracy left her feeling dissatisfied and unable to deliver what she wanted for her students. So when voluntary redundancies occurred she saw this as an opportunity to change direction and find something else that would give her a better sense of fulfilment. She joined her husband in his property development business.

When she describes Roger there is a mix of emotions around Marie; she describes him as being charismatic, powerful, confident and funny and you get a sense of how his optimistic and positive approach to life supported Marie on her way through her journey to discover who she was and what she was capable of. He created a truly safe environment where Marie felt secure to try new things and push herself; he told her he would always be there for her. Marie also has a huge sense of sadness about Roger.

They had bought two old dilapidated barns and, together with others, transformed them into magnificent properties – one of which Marie lives in. Her face lights up as she describes how she drove the digger and did many other physical jobs during the development, again liberating for her to see beyond her limitations. The sadness crosses her face when she tells me that Roger was diagnosed with cancer and only managed to live for another year after the properties were completed.

I can't image how this must have been for Marie, but you get a sense that the bottom fell out of her world. Her way of dealing with it initially was to suffer for the same period as Roger had twelve months of pain through his illness. She felt this was the least she could do, to somehow feel 'it' as he had felt 'it' for a year.

She became so sad that one day she decided to take her own life.

Life without Roger – her true soul mate – was something she could no longer endure.

Fortunately her time on this earth wasn't yet to end – she was found in time by her neighbours. What eventually dragged her from this awful dark and depressing state was her son Dan; she knew she couldn't inflict that pain on him again and she realised that he gave her a reason to carry on.

With Roger's death she felt she had lost her purpose in life; they had shared everything, even their work, and it seemed to Marie that she no longer had anything that gave her a reason to get up each morning. For someone whose life had been so driven, this was completely alien.

In a desire to find her purpose in life again she came across coaching and she enrolled to train as a coach – not fully understanding why, other than that she knew this would give her something each weekend to get up for. It took her out of her comfort zone and also gave her some everyday challenges to tackle. Booking hotels and getting to the places where the courses were being held, were all physical challenges that Roger would have supported her with. Having to find the solutions on her own reignited her internal drive to show herself what she was capable of, as she had done earlier in her life, although difficult, gave her a sense of familiarity.

The coaching didn't provide a future purpose for Marie but it did create a pathway from where she had been. She evolved, a different person, still sad, but more able to cope with her future journey through life. During this time she lost her mum and her father developed Alzheimer's, giving her yet another set of emotional and practical challenges to cope with. Being determined to continually move forward, neither of these, despite being very difficult, knocked her off course. Marie still didn't know where she was heading on the journey to regain her purpose, but she was dealing with all the knock-backs as they confronted her.

She hasn't wanted to sell her parents' home – should she have it as her home and move from the home she built with Roger, should she sell it? She was unclear. What she has done, and this gives you an idea of who Marie really is, she has given it to a struggling family to live in rent free for a year to give them time to get back on their feet.

Marie's purpose emerged in her desire to continue creating in the building world, as she had done with Roger. Exploring this further she bought a property in Cyprus that needed developing – it also gives her a bolt hole, as she describes it. She pushed herself to the limits and found a builder to support her in developing the property, which was full of disasters along the way. Just getting to Cyprus was a full scale challenge for Marie; being so independent, she liked to travel without having to rely on others for support. This meant she could only travel with a small bag strapped across her body; any clothes she decided to take with her she had to wear, layer upon layer.

Sorting out the travel arrangements, the building work and being in a foreign country where she was unable to speak the language really pushed Marie – the majority of able-bodied people wouldn't attempt such challenges. For Marie it was about pushing herself as she had done for the majority of her life – to show herself what she was capable of, returning to a way of being that felt familiar.

Marie shared with me a recurring dream that she has had throughout her life. In her dreams, she has no physical limitations, she is able to run freely in the countryside, and feel that anything is possible. Dreams give us messages and for Marie I am convinced that this was one that went to her subconscious and helped her find the way round her physical limitations, so that they were no longer there giving her an inner belief that whatever she attempted was possible.

Where is Marie now? On a journey to fully live her purpose – still wanting to be involved in property development, on her own or with a partner. She now has enjoyment in her life and is able to find happiness spending time with her grandchild, Joy, aptly named as she definitely brings joy into Marie's life and allows her to just be her best self, without feeling the need to always strive and push. She still holds her loss close but it is no longer consuming her.

Key areas of resilience that Marie demonstrated

This has been with her throughout her life; the early demonstrations as a child with that element of devilment within her, the ability to engage with others through humour, always helped her with aspects that were difficult. When she was consumed by grief for her husband, this strategy for coping left her.

Self-efficacy

Marie's strength of self-belief in her capabilities was immense and drove her to try all sorts of things in her life, intellectually and physically. Often comparison with others was the thing that was the catalyst for the next movement forward.

Purpose and sense of direction

There were times in Marie's story where this was really strong and propelled her forward, such as her desire to get a degree and then the promotion, with a clear idea of how she could impact positively on her students. Other times when this was not so clear to her or she felt it was so intertwined with her husband's that when he was no longer with her she felt she had lost it. During these times of loosing her purpose and direction, she also felt lost and wasn't sure of where she was going which curbed her normal enthusiasm and action orientated approach to life.

Problem solving, adaptability and a growth mindset

Marie was able always to keep her problems in perspective, she was never one to catastrophise an issue, she was able to see the problem for what it was and find a solution. The travel challenges she had throughout her story show that she found different ways to solve them. She was often curious to find out more about things, to learn more and have different experiences.

Support

Marie is good at helping others. Although not mentioned in the story, she often spent hours supporting her students with their problems so they could move forward. However she has found it difficult to ask others for what she needs, at times being over reliant on herself to solve a problem, her strong independence sometimes getting in the way. Other than with her husband, it was not natural to her to ask for help. She grew in this area when in America through allowing others, often through their American persistence, to support her when she hosted and had people stay.

Reminders for me through writing this chapter

We need to look beyond what we first see of a person. Otherwise we may never find out who they really are and what they are capable of.

Also, our past has a significant part to play in who we are today; it has shaped who we are, how we behave and who we believe we are. As a mother this is hugely significant and I'm grateful of the reminder to check how I am supporting the self-development of my children.

Strategies to help you develop your resilience – Marie-style

Humour

Viktor Frankl, survivor of the Nazi concentration camps, called humour 'another one of the soul's weapons in the fight for self-preservation'. He said that humour enabled him and others to rise above the barbarous circumstances of the camps for brief but precious periods.

Researchers Drs Shammi and Stuss, from the University of Toronto, studied people who endured damage to the frontal lobes of their right hemispheres. Their findings showed that these individuals were less able to process humour, reacting to it by smiling and laughing fewer times than the control group.

Train your right hemisphere through doing more creative activities, or relaxing the brain through meditation, breathing, yoga or just going out for a walk in the fresh air.

Humour is like a muscle, we need to exercise it and nurture it; listen to stand-up comedians, watch funny movies, read funny books, watch comedy TV, read the newspaper cartoon section, collect funny jokes that you can use to lighten the moment when with friends or relatives.

Find the funny side in everyday life, watch for and extract the 'funny', and humour will soon become more natural to you.

Adopt a humourous approach in life. If a problem occurs, try to see the funny side and learn to laugh at it.

Surround yourself with humour-loving people. Remember, the grouches will take you down their own misery spiral. Seek out the optimists, the positive people, and avoid the pessimists, the negative individuals.

If you hang out with fun-loving, optimistic and positive people, there is less chance of becoming depressed.

Learn to laugh at yourself and the ridiculous situations that occur from time to time.

Observe life, see the funny side, and make a note of it.

Talk more often; if you don't have a great sense of humour at the moment it may be because you're shy. Challenge yourself to talk to others, people you don't know, and make conversation.

Open up. Smile more often, and laugh even when something may not be funny. When you open yourself up, you will begin to see things you haven't seen before.

Self-efficacy

What do we mean by self-efficacy? Albert Bandura's definition is 'the belief in one's capabilities to organise and execute the courses of action to manage prospective situations'. In other words, self-efficacy is a person's belief in his of her ability to succeed in a particular situation. Bandura described these beliefs as determinants of how people think, feel and behave.

He developed a theory of self-efficacy which focused on four areas:

- Mastery experiences – things you have succeeded at in the past.
- Vicarious experiences – seeing people similar to you succeed.
- Social persuasion – hearing from others that you are capable.
- Emotional status – staying positive and managing stress.

Areas one, two and four are all in your area of control, and to a degree you can influence three by determining who you are around. Are they helpful supportive people or are they 'pickers' always identifying what's wrong with you or what you're not good at? These are not great people to be around when you are developing your self-efficacy or self-confidence. Choose who you want to be around that will be helpful and supportive.

Mastery experiences

A way of tapping into this experience is to write three successful and/or positive things that have happened at the end of each day. Another way is to look back at your successes and note down what you did and what skills and capabilities you used that enabled you to be successful. Being able to acknowledge and recognise our capabilities enables us to then use them going forward in different areas of our life. By jotting them down, when you are struggling with something and you can't seem to find the personal resources you need, you are able to look back over past successes and skills and this might just trigger what you need to do in the current situation.

Vicarious experiences

This was definitely a driver for Marie; she often looked at other people and what they were telling her and thought 'I can do that'. One technique is to find yourself a mentor, somebody who has maybe travelled a similar route and has reached a place or position that you would like to get to. Ask them how they did it, what tips they can give you and if they would be your mentor.

Mentoring is to support and encourage people to manage their own learning in order that they may maximise their potential, develop their skills, improve their performance and become the person they want to be. A mentor is usually more experienced and possibly older, who gives their personal support for no personal gain, although each mentoring experience has brought me increased self-learning. Mentoring tends to tap into an individual's desire to support others, which gives them a sense of fulfilment and satisfaction.

So think of somebody who you would like and ask them, think about why you would like them as your mentor and approach them. Most individuals enjoy helping and supporting others and you'll be surprised they might say yes.

I had a cheeky request via email from a lady called Donna, who was doing a managerial set of studies to support her career in healthcare; she had been asked to find a mentor, somebody who wasn't in her normal sphere. Donna approached me as I was a Non-executive Director at a different hospital. Her approach was cheeky but considerate and explained what she was looking for and why she was interested in seeing whether I would be interested. 'Great', I thought, 'somebody who is prepared to go out of their comfort zone, who understands the power of a mentor' and it was done in such a way that I couldn't really resist.

Another technique to tap into vicarious experiences is to identify people who you think are good at something you would like to be better at and use modelling. Modelling is an NLP technique which is really just about identifying how individuals do what they do well and you model yourself on that, copying their strategies.

Social persuasion

We have talked about social persuasion. Decide who is helpful to spend time, someone who is positive, supportive and up-beat. You know those people, the ones that are half glass full people, that always see the good and the positive in something rather than just being able to see what's wrong all the time. I didn't realise the impact of this until I was in the process of setting up my own business and leaving the corporate arena. There were those who I told about my ideas that were encouraging and supportive and were able to share their views on why I would be good at it, highlighting to me what others thought I had that people might be prepared to pay for. This was great, they helped motor me forward and reinforced my belief that I could do this. Then there were those that had a sapping effect, that made me question what I was doing, not in a helpful, that would be a good thing to think about way, but in a way that started to chip away at my self-confidence and made me start to question: 'could I really get it to work?' I had a coach at the time who got me to identify what the wobbles were and what the themes were and it was all about who I was interacting with. So for a period I spent less time with the people who weren't helpful and found more of those who were.

Purpose and clarity of direction

Marie kept pushing herself to learn more so she could deliver great teaching for her students. Understanding why you want to do something and tapping into your positive motivations really helps propel you forward and deal with the hard bits. It's the same for me writing this book, I enjoy the creative part, the research and the writing. However, the rereading and checking and rechecking and re-editing is something that drains me and I have to really discipline myself to do it, but understanding why it's important helps me connect again and deal with the bits I don't enjoy.

So ask yourself – 'why?' 'What's the bigger reason for doing this.' Help tap into your motivations and bigger reasons that help you through the difficulties.

The other thing Marie kept doing was setting herself challenges, pushing herself to achieve things, showing herself what she was capable of, which propelled her further forward as each success developed her confidence and self-belief.

Set yourself some small goals, gentle steps at first, ones that you know you can achieve; build your confidence and increase the personal challenge around your goals.

Your purpose doesn't have to be something big and significant and may change as you develop through your life. Marie's was initially about increasing her knowledge and intellect. It was about a thirst that couldn't be satisfied once she found it. She then moved into a joint purpose with her husband, which for her was again about learning and seeing what she was capable of. This theme of self-learning was picked up again when she trained as a coach, Marie's thirst for knowledge pushing her forward.

The message from Marie is that your purpose may meander along through life taking you to different situations and experiences that all develop who you are. Don't worry if it isn't always clear. Spend time on what you're interested in and what you enjoy. I was lucky enough when I was developing as a coach to work with a fellow coach on helping me identify my purpose. Working with others is useful to unlock what you hold within. My purpose is 'Joyfully inspiring growth'. I find this truly reflects who I am and what I do and gives me a good sense check when considering new things.

Problem Solving, adaptability and growth mindset

Try new things is the learning that comes from Marie – just do it. Give things a go, say 'yes' to opportunities that come your way.

Develop a love of learning. Ask lots of questions, explore, find out more. Nowadays there are so many ways in which you can develop your understanding of things from your armchair; with a laptop/smart phone you can access the web, read electronic books, watch videos and You Tube. You can go out into the world and have a small adventure as Marie did when she went to America. I recently wrote an article about Bilbo Baggins from *The Hobbit* and his initial resistance to extend his horizons beyond the Shire. However, once he stepped beyond the Shire his true learning began, proving fun, challenging and life changing. Plan an adventure for yourself.

Support

Marie found it difficult to ask for help but once she discovered that it wasn't connected to how others would see her limitations she was able to accept support more willingly. Do you resist support from others? If so, why? What is it the fear of? Explore your reasons. Understand them and then open yourself up gently to allow others to assist you.

Marie was also a great supporter of others. And she was a great role model, showing others what was possible despite her physical limitations. If you want to, you can. You just have to find a way. Her kindness to others was evident, to her students, her family, and her friends. Go about your daily life noticing others and offering assistance. Open the door for others, offer to help somebody in the supermarket. We often walk round not noticing. Open your eyes to others and see how you can help. Taking the focus off you and onto others helps put things into perspective and gets you to notice what you do have rather than what you don't have.

And finally, a friend found this poem and it reminded me of Marie. We hope you like it too.

I am Me. In all the world, there is no one else exactly like me. Everything that comes out of me is authentically mine, because I alone chose it — I own everything about me: my body, my feelings, my mouth, my voice, all my actions, whether they be to others or myself. I own my fantasies, my dreams, my hopes, my fears. I own my triumphs and successes, all my failures and mistakes.

Because I own all of me, I can become intimately acquainted with me. By so doing, I can love me and be friendly with all my parts. I know there are aspects about myself that puzzle me, and other aspects that I do not know — but as long as I am friendly and loving to myself, I can courageously and hopefully look for solutions to the puzzles and ways to find out more about me.

However I look and sound, whatever I say and do, and whatever I think and feel at a given moment in time is authentically me. If later some parts of how I looked, sounded, thought, and felt turn out to be unfitting, I can discard that which is unfitting, keep the rest, and invent something new for that which I discarded. I can see, hear, feel, think, say, and do. I have the tools to survive, to be close to others, to be productive, and to make sense and order out of the world of people and things outside of me.

I own me, and therefore, I can engineer me. I am me, and I am Okay.

Virginia Satir (American Psychologist and Educator, 1916-1988).

Chapter 3

JANE'S STORY – "THE POWER OF SELF-BELIEF"

Jane's story is about her strength of self-belief which enabled her to go through difficult times to get what she wanted. It helps us understand the power of combining a goal and a strong sense of belief – 'that it will happen'.

I first met Jane through her sister-in-law: they were running a consultancy business. Jane had two delightful children and was happily married with a strong network of friends. 'An ideal life' one might believe and, initially, so did Jane, until she explored the niggle, the something inside her that didn't feel quite right.

Before we open up this part of her story I want to share with you an earlier journey Jane made to achieve what she felt she was destined to be – this just amazed me.

Jane's early career took her into sales and marketing and she loved it, the culture being one of 'work hard and play hard', and did they play hard. You can imagine the brewing industry in the nineties when corporate entertainment was the norm and the expanse of events the company sponsored was extremely diverse – anything from music festivals to the 'Murphy's Oyster' event. With Jane being lucky enough to combine work with these exciting events, this was a dream job to have in your early twenties.

Her career developed nicely and she regularly got promoted and took on more responsibility. Her success was based on how she had built strong relationships both internally and externally with company clients; she had a varied diary – no two days were the same and it really didn't feel like work for much of the time. The environment was one of healthy competition between colleagues; she was rewarded through development and praise and this really worked well for Jane – bringing out the best in her performance.

Whilst she was working with her first brewing company there came a point when she felt that life was a little unfair. Despite receiving great praise, development opportunities and promotion, she compared what she was achieving against her male counterparts and, even though she recognised their length of service was longer than hers, she felt that the financial reward she had in comparison to them wasn't right. She couldn't do anything about that within the organisation and it took the edge off her performance as she became resentful. So, recognising this, she took action to move elsewhere and became National Accounts Manager for a different company. There, she really did start to think she had hit the big time. She was travelling to London two days a week to the head office and staying in posh hotels, which initially sweetened the early starts and long travel requirements. The company was young in terms of time in the UK. The team was also young and relatively small which meant a broader portfolio of responsibilities.

As time went on Jane recognised that the company's American culture didn't really bring out the best in her. Although she was happy and definitely did work hard to deliver results, the expectation to be in London for an 8 o'clock meeting on Mondays started to grate. The financial reward was good but she didn't feel nurtured or developed and negative feedback wasn't particularly handled in a constructive way. Basically they valued different things to her. Money and competition in an aggressive way didn't bring out the best in Jane.

It was whilst she was there that she, and Paul her husband, talked about having a family. Taking the sensible approach the plan was to come off the pill for three months and completely get all the chemicals out of her body before they would actively start trying. This was the plan and Jane expected no issues along the way – she was well organised and had learnt that planning and action generally meant success.

Her disquiet with the business and her future plans about becoming a mother made Jane start to think about where might be a better place to work. She put a few feelers out with people she knew and got offers from two different directions. One opportunity was with an old colleague who had left the brewing industry and moved into IT and the other was back at her first company. Jane knew believing in the brand was important to her and she was also starting to understand what environment worked best for her, so these two factors, as well as just loving the brewing industry, sent her back to her original brewing company as Regional Sales Manager. What also attracted her to this position was the fact that this would give her a new challenge of learning all about line management and would be a good addition to her CV.

Changing career and trying for a baby wasn't daunting to Jane – everything would work out as it was meant to be, was her motto. At the same time as deciding to start her own family, Jane's oldest school friend was also on this same journey. They shared stories and excitement about what their lives would be like with their new babies and what they would do together. Her friend got pregnant and Jane was delighted and thought 'great, me next'. But it never seemed to happen.

At work all was going really well. Jane enjoyed the responsibilities of management, she enjoyed her team and other work colleagues and was having a great time. However, she started to notice that she was becoming two people – one person at home, trying to become a mother, and another person at work, fully concentrating on the job. Upon waking she would feel down about not being pregnant, but once at work managed to be in a whole different world where she was totally occupied. Eventually, however, she and her husband decided they should consider seeking advice.

With this in mind a trip to the doctor's was arranged and luckily the one they saw had an interest and expertise in fertility so quickly sent them both off for tests to see if they could find any problem. To Jane this was nothing, it would be easily sorted and she would then become pregnant. Unfortunately the results came back with problems on both sides and the doctor advised them to go onto IVF. This was a huge shock to Jane.

She talked herself through this and got to a place that was 'well this is the route to getting me pregnant and give us our baby'. Believing that IVF must be the solution enabled her to say 'yes, let's do it'.

At work she only spoke about this to her line manager, who was exceptionally supportive. Jane wanted to keep this part of her life separate from her 'corporate career woman' role. This enabled her to focus on the work she probably instinctively knew would help her cope with difficulties that might arise with the new challenges in her personal life.

Despite the fact that IVF was extremely emotional, and at times undignified, Jane 'knew' it would lead to her being pregnant and getting their baby and this got her through it. Also work was a great escape. Taking some control and doing something positive toward what she and Paul wanted helped her feel that things were happening.

Following all the preceding procedures Jane had her eggs placed back in her womb and almost immediately she 'felt' pregnant. She walked more cautiously; she sat down more tentatively; she got the taste of metal in her mouth and other little symptoms which appeared to reinforce her belief that she was pregnant.

However, she wasn't. All these were imaginary symptoms which she had read about and were embedded in her subconscious. Because her belief in becoming pregnant was so strong she had physically experienced them. She felt her world had fallen apart when she discovered she wasn't expecting.

Jane wanted action immediately to get them back on track to becoming parents, but medically a two week interval is necessary before restarting a new set of IVF treatment. This was an eternity to her; it was stealing time which she would then miss out on with her baby. Despite all this going on in the background she got promoted at work; her career was going well and continued to be a means of strength and an enjoyable distraction during this difficult time.

They had another go at freezing her eggs and because Jane had such a belief that this would lead them to what was rightfully theirs, a baby, that strength of feeling that this was meant to be her way to get her baby kept her going through the dark and difficult times.

At work she faced even more challenges as she was now a Field Sales Controller and, being at a higher level, the challenges were more strategic. Thank goodness she loved it; she describes this position with a smile on her face as being the best corporate role she ever had. The stimulation, the challenge, the responsibility to manage and develop others, whilst looking ahead into the future with her peers and identifying the best way forward for the organisation, was the mental challenge that enabled her to forget the very difficult things going on at home.

Jane was being pumped with drugs, which were getting harder to endure, and further failures occurred. Her belief was still that she was going to be a mother and 'bad things don't happen to me, this is just a blip I need to work through'.

Jane ended up with six attempts at freezing her eggs and four full attempts at IVF, over an 18 month period. Each intervention whittled away at her energy and general happiness in life. Not surprisingly this became her complete focus when not at work.

For anybody who has been in this situation, you will recognise the fact that you see pregnant women everywhere. You spend your days knowing you need to do something to take your pain away but find it difficult to summon the energy to do so. When not at work she found immediate satisfaction in spending money on clothes, hoping it would fill the gap of not having a child. Jane and her husband spent weekends away with friends going through a similar situation, visiting spas, generally spending money to try to comfort themselves. It didn't really work – there might have been short term satisfaction but the 'gap' in their life was still evident. Looking back, she realises that quite a lot of the clothes she bought she never actually wore. They just hung in the wardrobe, lifeless, which is how she felt at this time. Her identity of being a mother was not being fulfilled and it left a huge whole in her life.

During this difficult time her best friend, who she was exceptionally close to, became pregnant for a second time. This just didn't seem fair to Jane and she took it very badly – really feeling sorry for herself, as it heightened what she hadn't got. So intense were these feelings within her that she wrote her friend a letter saying that she would no longer be able to be see her and be around her as she thought their lives were going in different directions and it was too difficult for her. All the things they had once spoken about doing together, when they both had their children, no longer seemed possible. Throughout this time Jane found herself keeping a distance from all her friends who had children; it was just too much of a painful reminder of what was missing in her life. Instead she sought refuge with others she felt understood her pain, other potential mothers going through IVF.

As you would imagine, this period of her life was emotionally dark, she cried a lot, she withdrew from others, and this was out of character for Jane who is a sociable, friendly individual who makes time for social occasions.

The IVF process had become a new way of being and with each failure it was becoming harder to muster up the energy and get through the disappointment. After the last time it hadn't worked Jane was mentally getting herself prepared for another session, when her consultant delivered some devastating news: he believed that after all the failed attempts IVF wasn't going to be successful for them – no matter how much money they paid for further treatment. This was like a physical blow to Jane and she found it hard to comprehend the reality of what the consultant had said to her.

As you can imagine, she wasn't able to sleep that night and needing to work towards achieving her goal, she set about finding another possible route to becoming a mother. She got out of bed at 2am and researched all night everything there was to know about adoption. When her husband woke in the morning she delivered this as the next possible option for them. Her desire to have a family was so strong that she knew this had to be the route.

She rang the adoption agency. 'Let's get moving and take action' is a theme that has been evident throughout Jane's life – if she is in control and taking action to move forward, she feels that she is making progress towards her goal.

Having read all there was to read about adoption she knew that the advice is that after IVF people are asked to wait for six months. This was not an option for Jane; it was time that she thought should be with her child not just hanging around waiting.

They managed to pass the first hurdle on the race to get through the adoption route more quickly. After their initial visit, which was in the summer, they were asked to attend preparation groups, but not until November. For Jane this again was madness —she wanted to get on with it all 'now'.

At this stage she reconnected with her friends who already had children, feeling that she could talk to them about this. Jane also gained support from her family. The preparation courses were great in painting the worst-case scenario and managing expectations that there weren't many babies, but Jane's positive belief that she would find her child made her strong and energised by this new process.

The next phase was called home study, where you work closely with a social worker exploring your childhood and your close relationships; this is emotional but quite cathartic. It also made her realise how special her parents were in creating the amazing childhood she had had. She understood more around her feelings and emotions during the IVF treatment and shared these with Paul, enabling them to get a deeper understanding of each other through that difficult IVF time.

One of the most challenging conversations to have was on what type of child they felt they could parent. Jane was so desperate to have one, she had to pass the test, so she thought she ought to say 'any type of child' – not wanting to limit her chances. She did manage to say that she would prefer a child between birth and four, but the whole 'disabled' discussion was exceptionally difficult for her with these internal conflicts going on: – would she pass the test, did she really think she could mother a disabled child.

Jane realised that the social worker was an extremely skilled individual who enabled her to honestly express what she felt would be the best option for her and Paul without feeling she had ruined her chances and failed the test.

The stakes were really high now – this was the only route to becoming parents for Jane and Paul. At times she was exceptionally angry at having to be tested; she would be a great mother, couldn't they see this? Her anger was also about the time it was taking. And there was fear that the adoption option would be removed. The pressure of feeling judged all the time was wearing, making them tired and low; sometimes Jane questioned her self-belief that she would be a good mother.

The next big hurdle was when they got through to panel, which is where they were interviewed by ten people who assess the reports and assessments which had been gathered to date.

This was the scariest thing Jane had ever had to go through. Ten people sitting round a room judging her and determining how her future may go. The stakes were so high that she couldn't even contemplate failure. Great news – they were approved to be adoptive parents. When Jane rang her parents in a state of euphoria, her dad's response to this was 'well of course you got approved', reiterating the belief in his daughter that she would make a great mum and 'what was all the fuss about'.

A family was becoming a reality because they now had the go-ahead for Social Services to match them to a child needing parents.

Another long wait . . .

Despite continuing to enjoy work and knowing that in time they would have a child, Jane found it difficult to sit and wait. There was nothing she could do to move things forward, no more hurdles to prepare for, no more tests to pass. Her belief about becoming a mother began to waver as she couldn't see what she could do to get closer to it.

One day driving home from a conference she thought to herself "This is rubbish", "I'm fed up". She got home feeling flat and down, willing herself to carry on with work which would take her mind off it but as she walked in the door the phone went it was Mark, her social worker, to tell her they had a match - a girl, nine months old.

After the call she rang Paul in hysterics – all she told him was that he needed to get home *now* in between the sobs which were all Paul heard of the message before she hung up on him. Paul was unable to get back in contact to check what the matter was as she was then phoning everybody to tell them the great news. Paul got home not knowing what on earth was the matter with his wife, not at all expecting her to tell him the fantastic news.

Jane and Paul read the baby's file and just knew that she was meant to be their daughter.

Of course, after this, work lost its attraction; it was no longer important; now it was all about the excitement of having a daughter.

In Jane's head, they were back into tests as the social worker for Ellie, the baby identified as requiring adoptive parents, came to meet Jane and Paul. She thought: 'we might fail; they might take our daughter away from us'. The same fears crept in when they met Ellie's foster mother. At this meeting Jane saw photos of Ellie; she was beautiful. The months of waiting, the IVF treatments, now crept up on Jane and tears rolled down her face in disbelief that she was looking at a picture of her daughter.

The process there on was not plain sailing. When applying for a 'freeing order' the biological parents contested and this delayed things by another three months. Then there was a final panel to formally approve the match and again Jane feared that it could all be pulled away from her.

At last, approval!

After all the formalities, Jane and Paul were able to meet their daughter, going to see her in the foster home, learning about her different routines, all building up to being able to take her out and eventually bring her home.

On the first visit, Jane was in such a state that she was hyperventilating, part of her not believing she was about to meet her daughter for the first time. When they walked in and saw her, Ellie turned round and gave them a huge smile. Jane fell to the floor crying with relief, happiness and an inner knowing that this was what she had been striving for, for so long.

Visits went on for five days, each time having to walk away and leave Ellie with her foster mother. Jane's emotions were all over the place, trying to be sensitive to the foster mother's feelings as she had had Ellie for a long period of time and was clearly fond of her. But at last Ellie did come home. You may think this was the end of Jane's journey to become a mother, all the trauma she had put herself through to achieve her desire of becoming a mum and fulfilling her identity. But Jane had her heart set on two children so in typical style she started the process again 12 months later.

Despite knowing the routine and route and rationalising the past, her emotions were like a roller coaster again. But she got an early Christmas present of a phone call from Mark, the same social worker, to let her know that they had another match: Dylan, an 18-month-old boy. All went well and he is now established within the family.

When her 12 month leave was due to end after adopting Ellie, Jane did really not want to return to work and she was also starting the journey of finding their second child. As luck would have it, they had a restructure at work which enabled Jane to take voluntary redundancy. She knew this was the right thing as she knew instinctively that her life in the corporate world was over. She felt she might work again, and probably knew that financially she would have to, but for now she could rethink what that might be, whilst enjoying being a mum — savouring what had taken her a difficult time to achieve.

Recognising Jane's marketing and managerial skills, her father-in-law and sister-in-law, who were in business together, tentatively approached Jane to see if she would be interested in working temporarily with them on a part-time basis. After a successful initial period they asked her to join them as a partner. Jane agreed but only on the basis that it was part time.

It was during her time in this new position that Dylan arrived. The business was small so Jane didn't have the luxury of 12 months off, but she agreed to take two months and then return again part time. Although this seemed logical, and Dylan appreciated the mental stimulus of going to nursery for three days a week, Jane wasn't ready to return, but she didn't realise this until much later on. She can now look back and understand why she found aspects of work difficult at that time. It was the internal pull emotionally, conflicting with where she was.

This led to her feeling guilty — that she wasn't being the same kind of mum to Dylan as she had been to Ellie, that she wasn't handling Dylan as well as she had Ellie, that her business partner felt she wasn't pulling her full weight within the business. All this guilt ate away at her and really prevented her dealing with things in her normal proactive way. Frustrations came out in the work environment and also some resentment for feeling like this. Jane and her partner's ability to explore these feelings was not good, her partner had her own tensions and frustrations and these weren't explored or explained. All of this resulted in snipes, neither of them fully pulling together on the joint purpose of the business; emotions and frustrations were bubbling and getting in the way of what was possible from a work perspective and way forward.

When Jane returned from leave after Dylan's arrival, her father-in-law had retired, leaving her sister-in-law and herself as the partners in the business. In principle this seemed logical, however their spats continued, nothing major, but they were there. Jane was conscious that she owed her partner for the time she had had off with Dylan and that she was able to work part time so she felt she should be grateful. This often prevented her from expressing how she really felt.

Jane's father-in-law worked with me as his coach to help him develop a retirement plan. He had attempted retirement three times previously and ended up returning to full-time work each time. On this occasion he wanted to retire but felt he needed some support to ensure he was successful.

We developed a clear exit strategy and afterwards Jane and her partner thought it might be useful to explore how I did that and also learn more about the personality profiling I offered through my business. They were recognising that independent support might help them both with the issues they had between them.

I volunteered to profile them both and do one-to-one feedback sessions initially to help them raise their self-awareness. This resulted in a joint session helping them understand the differences and needs of each other as identified through the profiling. This created a light bulb moment for them both – understanding the differences between them through this objective process helped unlock what was going on.

Jane also asked for some individual coaching, initially to help her explore the internal conflict she was having between work and home. In one of the sessions Jane defined what she wanted to do with the whole of her life; by allowing her imagination to flow and not be constrained in her thinking, she spilled out that she would love to work part time as a social worker. As it came out there was a sense of relief from Jane, being able to share the desire of wanting to do something more meaningful to her than the role she was currently in, where the opportunity for part-time flexible work had got in the way of her realising how she really felt about the job and potentially what was missing.

The fact was that the current work didn't mean anything to her, she wasn't passionate about it, it wasn't important in her world.

Jane, if I had allowed her to, would have put this dream firmly back in her head and sunk it deep within her as she felt logically this was not an option – how could she at her age become a social worker? I encouraged her to take small steps to explore what was involved and what were the routes to becoming one

The more she spoke to others about the possibilities and different routes to qualify, the more it fuelled her passion for the role. A key influencer was her social worker Mark, who had supported her through both adoptions, from whom she was able to get a 'reality' point of view and explore the current routes in. Mark also shared his view that he thought she would be excellent as a social worker. Having that encouragement from someone she admired and respected made her believe this was potentially possible.

Jane then worked on a goal map, encompassing all the aspects she would need to take into consideration in making this dream happen – everything from her personal health and energy, through to finances and finding the right way for her to get qualified. This became daunting and she quickly built a brick wall of excuses and reasons for not taking this further. I asked her to metaphorically push one brick out in the wall and to look through it. I asked her what could she see through the wall? How would she feel if she was at the other side of that wall? After tapping into her positive emotions around this desire I asked her what the 'brick' was that she pushed through and how might she push it away in reality. (Metaphors are great ways to explore individual's dreams and fears as they are initially 'removed' from them until you reconnect it back in, but describing it through the metaphor helps people find their solutions).

With each brick Jane found a way to push it over until the wall was so low that she was able to walk over it and through into a world of new possibilities. Exploring what her perceived blockers were and finding solutions refuelled her passion; it was no longer just about being a social worker, this was about a career where she could see herself in the future combining her management and leadership skills with the training and aspects she would learn and have a career where she was passionate and truly believed in what she was doing.

One of the blockers was how would she share this change of direction with her sister-in-law who had enabled her to have a part-time role in the business partnership. They had made so much progress as a team with their relationship and understanding of each other. Through exploring what might be her sister-in-law's fears and concerns, Jane was better prepared for this conversation. Although still difficult, a good outcome was ensured and the relationship then just strengthened.

Really planning for this conversation and looking at it from a different perspective helped remove the emotion and make it an objective and supportive exercise. It enabled them to explore the concerns with the business openly and have a strategy to deal with the impact of Jane potentially leaving.

Jane's next worry was whether she would be able to get on a university course, bearing in mind the youthful competition she would be up against. Her belief in herself began to waver. We changed the language and I got her to think of herself as a Social Worker, exploring what they would do and how they would feel, really sitting in their world and sensing it. These subtle changes enabled her to rebuild that self belief about her own ability and that this was going to happen. She truly believed she was meant to be a mother and was prepared to go through the difficulties to reach that goal, which took her to happiness and becoming a mother. So getting her to believe she was a good social worker would help her through this difficulty.

Jane was given an interview for the course she wanted at Sheffield University. To prepare her we did some visualisation in which she 'experienced' a successful in interview, living it in advance.

This is a great technique to tap into when you have an important meeting or interview – visualise what it will be like. It impacts on your subconscious brain enabling you to reaccess it in the actual situation later.

To really strengthen her positive emotions and feel a relaxed happiness, we 'anchored' a powerful past experience in Jane's body, one she could then access at any time. This enabled her to be in a resourceful state for the interview.

After being accepted onto the social worker course, Jane began doing practical work with reoffenders and thoroughly enjoyed it. She became alive again. The new learning reinvigorated her and despite it being hard and challenging, because of the necessary assignments, her enjoyment and self-belief carried her forward one step at a time through her qualifications.

She is now a fully qualified social worker and a mum for Jane true fulfilment.

Key areas of resilience demonstrated by Jane

Self-efficacy

Jane's belief about her being a mother was exceptionally strong and enabled her to get through the difficult set backs. However her belief around being a social worker was not as strong and resulted in her having major doubts. We had to work hard at getting her to really feel that the possibility for her to become a social worker was possible and that she was able to become one.

Optimism

Despite many emotional knock-backs, Jane picked herself up and knew she would find a solution to deliver her purpose – being a mother. When her optimism wavered in connection with becoming a social worker, we used a number of techniques to reconnect her with a more positive view point.

Purpose and clarity of direction

Jane's purpose was crystal clear around her becoming a mother. She knew the route to get there. When difficulties occurred she was so connected to where she was going that she found alternative solutions.

Problem solving, adaptability and growth mindset

Within her workplace Jane had grown, learnt more about herself and found new solutions to problems. Being highly action-oriented she knew that finding different approaches was key to her success. She took this approach to her personal life and was prepared to find alternatives through adapting and learning more. When she was solving problems and taking action she was in control and reassured through her belief in herself. When she was waiting for things to happen this disempowered her and often had a negative impact on her emotions.

Reminders for me through writing this chapter

Despite the knock-backs, Jane didn't give up. She knew she was meant to be a mother. Having this powerful connection around who you are and what you do powers you through difficult times. That strength of purpose and clarity enabled Jane to find alternative solutions and gave her energy to move forward despite difficulties. Taking time to fully understand your purpose and future direction will reap huge benefits in your success to achieve.

This was similar for me around writing this book. Initially I seemed clear on the direction and purpose. Then somewhere in the middle I lost direction and my energy waned and I didn't make much progress. In fact I got a bit disillusioned with it and all those self-doubts crept back in. Who was I to write a book, etc? Having spent time connecting with why I was wanting to do this and getting clarity, it opened up the door as to what I needed to do next. So the big lesson for me is truly explore your bigger sense of direction and purpose.

Strategies to develop resilience Jane-style

Self-efficacy

Jane's practice at work was to take time at planning things, understanding her options, researching them and then planning the order of events and what success looked like. She took this approach to her personal life too. When she was able to plan and take control it reinforced her belief she would be successful. It was down to her so what could she do? Covering off all the aspects built her confidence level around her ability to be successful. Take time out to plan your approach; preparation brings a state of mind where things seem possible.

Draw from your past, take time to consider what successes you have had, explore how you accomplished them. Reconnect with what you did to make it possible. Recognise what you're capable of. Through connecting with Jane's success around becoming a mother, I unlocked some blockers for Jane around what was possible and how she could use her talents and skills when other challenges arose.

Optimism

See yourself as the cause, not the effect. You don't have to be a product of your circumstances. Jane didn't dwell on the unfairness around how she couldn't become a mother. She constantly rethought what she could do about her situation. She constantly set new goals and found new solutions.

Remember, life is short. Jane was constantly concerned about the delays on her journey to becoming a mother. The same was true once she committed to being a social worker. How could she get there quickly? She knew that taking action and making things happen would make the difference. There was no benefit in brooding and spending time being pessimistic or down. Yes, she felt knocked and disappointed but she took control and made decisions to move on in a different direction. Pessimism breeds indecision. You dwell on things that haven't happened and aren't a reality. Remind yourself this is your life and that you have the power to positively move forward to make the most of the time you have. Ask yourself, if you knew you only had 12 months left to live a healthy life, what would you do? How can you make more of that happen now? Live the life you want.

Purpose and clarity of direction

Having a clear sense of who you are and what you want to achieve helps propel you forward – especially through difficulties, as with Jane. She knew she was a mother. This enabled her to find extra strength and energy when she had the setbacks. Here are some questions for you to consider for yourself.

- Who are you?
- What's important to you?
- What's your personal mission in life?

An exercise might be to develop your own Mission Statement.

Step 1   Identify your values   (ref page 101 in Clare's story under the strategies – purpose and direction).

Step 2   Understand what your values in action look like.

Step 3   Take time to write your personal mission. It should encompass your values and how you'd like to express them in your life. The statement can be as long or as short as you want. You can come back and critique it. But start by putting pen to paper and see what comes out.

Problem solving, adaptability and growth mindset.

Jane had many different approaches to her problem solving, each situation giving her feedback around what didn't work. It was a learning opportunity which helped her identify a new and different way forward.

Be clear on what exactly the problem is, rather than generalising or making the problem bigger than it really is. 'What exactly is the problem and why is it a problem?' Helps get to the nub. Once you have clarity you know what you are dealing with and can then explore alternative solutions.

Research. Jane found out all there was to know to help inform her choices so she knew how to make those new options work for her.

Around the glimmer idea of becoming a social worker she went and spoke to her own social worker, asking lots of questions to find out as much as possible. She spoke to people at the university to understand more about the process of getting onto the course, informing her how she could better prepare herself. Explore through discussing with others, don't close things down; open things up through learning more.

Your time is limited, so don't waste it living someone else's life. Don't be trapped by dogma – which is living with the results of other people's thinking. Don't let the noise of others' opinions drown out your own inner voice. And most important, have the courage to follow your heart and intuition. They somehow know what you truly want to become. Everything else is secondary. – Steve Jobs.

Chapter 4

SARAH'S STORY – "REDISCOVERING WHO I AM"

Sarah, in her early forties, was happily married with a son in his early teens. Her husband was a successful business executive who often travelled with business.

Earlier in her life, and because her son didn't need her so much, the challenges Sarah faced were around what to do as a career – what would stimulate her and give her a sense of fulfilment. She found that career direction then and trained as a teacher; the commercial experience she had gained prior to the birth of her son really helped her and she excelled in this new profession.

But her relationship with her husband was beginning to falter. He travelled extensively and was often tired and didn't want to enjoy life in the way they had previously. They were growing into different people through their work and through life in general; they were no longer the youngsters they had been when they first got together at university. Sarah was often at home, supporting their son, and waiting for her husband to return from one of his trips, not consciously aware but somehow feeling that something was missing.

From the outside, Sarah's life looked pretty much on track. She had the support of loving friends whom she socialised with, either alone or with her husband. Her career was going well and she enjoyed what she was doing. Life was full with family, friends and work.

Then Sarah hit a stumbling block. She became concerned about her marriage – but not unduly, she was still having fun with her husband;

hadn't they only just been on a trip with friends to New York and enjoyed fun, laughter and sex? But Sarah sensed something was wrong and one weekend whilst with friends she shared her fears. She sat on her friend's bed and cried, weeks of worry and concern at feeling something wasn't right but not wanting to see it, flooded out. She had noticed changes in her husband: he was distant and she didn't feel it was just work; he had become super fit and exercised a lot; his travel had now started to encroach on special family and friends occasions, which it had never done before. She sensed that she had lost her husband – that he was seeing someone else. She spoke those words out loud for the first time and this is when the tears came. Sharing her fears with somebody else made them seem real, rather than her own concern.

Her husband had left their friends early to go to a business function.

So Sarah was able to discuss her concerns and gain reassurance and support; just having somebody to listen to her was helpful. This was something that she had missed terribly – her husband had been a wonderful friend and support through many difficult times in their life together but recently he had not been there for her. Would she have been able to discuss her concerns with him on this particular occasion? Probably not.

After arriving home, Sarah needed to know for sure what was going on.. She couldn't live like she was any more, with this fear and not knowing for real.

She found herself doing something she had never done before, compelled to do it to help her find the truth. She rummaged through her husband's bags, with the excuse to herself of finding his dirty washing for the washer.

And there it was, the evidence . . .

She felt sick and angry. Half of her had hoped that her senses were wrong and she wouldn't find anything but this was something that she couldn't ignore. It was there in front of her, tormenting her, making her face the truth. Now, having found out, she knew that her life would no longer be the same again.

What had she found? A condom packet. She was on the pill so she knew this was not for her benefit.

Her fears had become reality and wishing to sort out their problems – to work through this crisis – she confronted him. Although angry she didn't show her anger, but asked outright if he was seeing somebody else. This calmness surprised her but helped her move forward and deal with what was going on between them honestly. He didn't deny it, he didn't explain it, but it just hung in the air between them for a while.

Sarah still loved her husband despite what he had done; there was so much history and life they had shared together that she felt that maybe they could work through this and come out the other side together. But she knew that a relationship with three people in it was not one she could cope with. Hoping that he would feel the same she asked him if he could give the other woman up so they could work things out.

Devastatingly for Sarah, her husband said he couldn't. This felt like a physical blow taking the air from her lungs. He didn't want to work through this problem with her as they had done with other difficulties in their lives. And they had been through a lot.

Since university Sarah had hardly known any life without having her husband at her side, but she made a strong and difficult decision that if he couldn't give up the other woman then their marriage was over. He had shut down the way forward together.

We now look at Sarah's journey further on in life. She is an inspiration to others in what she has achieved. On reflection, her story is also a great example of an NLP 'presupposition' – every action has a positive intention. Often we don't realise this until much later and I think Sarah would agree that, three years on, she is a much different person to the one she was then.

After the devastating news she heard from her husband, Sarah physically collapsed, unable to walk. The shock and enormity of the situation hit her like a thunderbolt. Yes, she had had an idea that things weren't right and confronted it in a dignified manner to protect her son but she had in no way prepared herself for what would come as a result of the question she asked. Her husband was choosing someone else.

Sarah's journey is one of self-discovery — somehow she found the Sarah that had become lost in the marriage.

How did she get started? How did she pull herself out of a place so full of despair that she couldn't even describe it? Well, she was able to ask for help and she accepted that she needed help. She was catapulted into a place she had no previous experience of dealing with — a totally foreign land with nothing that looked or felt familiar. Her best friend and lover was no longer by her side to support her and work it out together as they had done with other difficulties in their lives.

Sometimes in life we are lucky enough to have a fairy godmother or two looking out for us and supporting us in our difficult dark times. Sarah found crucial people to lean on and guide her through this haze. Her younger sister took control when Sarah collapsed. Sarah had brought her sister up from a young age as their mother and father died when she was still young and Sarah had not long finished university. Initially her Sister was unable to get Sarah out of bed, her body had just shut down from the shock and she was not able to get her physical functions operating. A doctor's visit was arranged. Getting Sarah medical support and assistance was the first step forward.

Somewhere in that haze, Sarah knew she didn't want to be like others she had known when their husbands had left. In short, she was not going to be a victim; she knew she wanted to find happiness again and she believed that she would. These thoughts were lost initially and as medication enabled her to function again and she accepted the support of others, her role as a mother kicked back in. It was important to her that her son felt supported. He had been let down by his father, the person who he relied upon, looked up to, but who had now hurt his mother so badly that she found it difficult to not cry or function initially.

This amazing strength of character and positive spirit moved Sarah from where she was to where she is today. She was clear she wanted to be as far away as possible from the painful place she was in.

All of us are generally pain or pleasure types of people — either moving away from pain or towards pleasure. Some of us are stimulated into action because we are moving away from painful situations. If this is the case for you or someone you know, how painful does the pain have to be before movement away from it is created? And for those amongst us who are stimulated by pleasure, we can create a fantastic picture of where we want to be, how we want it to be, and we can imagine it to be so exciting that we compel ourselves to go out and find it.

Initially Sarah's main focus was her son, along with work; she wanted to get back to some sort of normality. Being able to think of others for some time during the day, and not just about what was missing in her life, or tying herself up in negative thoughts about what she had done wrong in her relationship, enabled Sarah to build back her strength slowly and surely. She got to a situation where she wanted to make positive movement forward rather than just surviving and managing to live with the dulled pain.

Sarah knew she wanted more and as she had had more in her life, was able to recognise that it might be possible again to find future happiness.

Sarah identified that she had lost some of her identity whilst in the marriage and she had compromised around things that used to be important to her. This is where she started on her rediscovery of happiness –reconnecting with who she really was rather than 'the wife'.

Not knowing exactly what she wanted, other than something more than what she had, and not really understanding where she had ended up and who she now was, she created a vision board. This taps into the subconscious pictorially around what we might want to do and what we are seeking.

Sarah chose a picture of an attractive, confident-looking female who looked happy sitting in a piazza somewhere in Italy. When we explored this image to see what this meant to her, she described how the woman looked so 'at one with herself', enjoying her own company in a beautiful place. She also looked calm, comfortable and generally enjoying life.

This unlocked quite a lot for Sarah: she realised she had lost confidence in doing things by herself. She had always done things with her husband, her sister or with friends. Even having a cup of coffee somewhere on her own filled her with uncertainty and concern. In exploring the meaning behind the image we were able to come up with some simple and small steps which took her nearer to what she wanted for herself.

Sarah took her first step, and went for a coffee by herself. She then started to get used to the idea of being alone and realised that, actually, she was great company and that it was OK to become used to that.

As time went on we also explored that, as a girl, Sarah had loved the ballet, but had never been as a grown woman because her husband didn't like it. So, one day a big goal popped up in Sarah's head – she fancied going to the Royal Opera House to see *Swan Lake*. How great would she feel if she were to achieve this goal for herself?

Scared? Absolutely!

Here was a woman who for so many years had identified herself only as one half of a partnership and had given little thought to who Sarah herself was throughout all of that time. She now felt that the Sarah she had been once had somehow got lost along the way, and was quite surprised when she started to look back at all the fantastic qualities the 'old' Sarah had possessed. She had changed from the girl she was in her earlier years at university – the girl who was independent, confident, fun and had a real sense of purpose and excitement about the future.

Sarah set herself the challenge of realising her goal to visit the Opera House and luckily *Swan Lake* was on in the early summer that year. She booked the ticket and then went though the usual collywobbles, familiar to us all.

We worked on what Sarah would wear, travel arrangements, how the evening would go, what she would do at the interval and, very importantly, what Sarah would feel like once she had achieved this big step. As a coach, my job was to help Sarah get a real sense of how she would feel once she had achieved this major goal.

When the big day arrived Sarah overcame the apprehension she felt and went to the ballet – on her own. And how did she feel once she had done it? Amazing – not only had she achieved a life long ambition to go to the Royal Ballet but had done it on her own and enjoyed herself. This allowed her to feel more confident and comfortable with herself and was another step in moving her towards the woman in her picture.

Sarah's working life has seen some progression also in the last couple of years. She could have taken the easy route and stayed in the primary school where she was recognised as being a good teacher. But she was no longer growing personally and there were no goals to stretch her or push her capabilities to the next level.

Her view might have been, 'I've got enough on my plate at the moment, I should push this thought away, deep inside, and ignore it', but Sarah chose to explore the feelings she was experiencing – what was she seeking that her current position didn't give her?

She realised that she needed a new challenge, something to stimulate her, creating an element of excitement with just a smidgen of apprehension at the same time. An opportunity arose for her to teach Advanced Skills to other teachers and through this transition she raised her self-esteem and showed herself just what she was capable of. She acknowledged what she is good at and recognised her talents. Sarah has the ability to make others feel great and achieve more than they think they are capable of. This, combined with her skills as a teacher, started to generate great results with the teachers she was allocated to support, encourage and raise their teaching ability.

Whilst Sarah was developing courage and belief in her own ability, she was helping struggling teachers to raise their belief and personal confidence too – often resulting in them achieving increased assessment grades when monitored by Ofsted.

Was Sarah's journey of rediscovery all plain sailing? No. She had a few knock-backs. One situation physically knocked her off her bike. She had decided in one of the sessions that exercise and the outdoors were going to be important to her. As a younger woman she had cycled a lot, so out came the bike and sometimes she went out alone and other times she went with her sister who was still around offering friendly support and company. On one such ride a car knocked her off her bike and carried on without stopping. Luckily Sarah had a helmet on. A gentleman, a doctor it turned out, stopped to see how she was and whether there were any serious injuries, which luckily there weren't. I remember this story because Sarah told it with humour, relating how her sister had pointed out that the doctor was rather good looking and that she'd wasted the opportunity to play the dying swan and make the most of a good-looking gentlemen coming to her rescue.

Humour is a great healer. Being able to see the funny side of something and laugh enables you to release the natural endorphins that make us feel good. So despite the physical pain she was in and the emotional wounds she was healing, Sarah was getting to a stage where laughter, which had always been a part of her, was once again returning.

Sarah's son was an important part of her journey back. It was important to her that she gave him a place where he could show his emotions and share how he felt about his dad. Being a teenager, it was important, she felt, that he be encouraged to talk. Sarah tried to handle this with dignity, balancing honesty with having in her mind that she wanted her son to still have a relationship with his father. This enabled her to have conversations with her son that didn't involve her criticising or blaming or being angry at her husband. These conversations were about what was right for her son, not what she needed. It's not that she didn't get angry and didn't shout at her husband over financial difficulties that started to arise but she didn't show this to her son, not wanting to tarnish his relationship with his dad even further.

This sense of purpose around the conversations enabled her to reflect on the good times she and her husband had had, and that just because the relationship had ended it didn't mean that their time together hadn't been anything other than happy; they had been in love and shared some fantastic moments together. Their lives had just gone in different directions and her husband had decided to take a different route to the one she was on. This sense of perspective around her relationship enabled her to see the situation for what it was rather than it tainting everything they had had together.

The final part of Sarah's journey shows her strength of character and desire to be with someone in the future. In fact it was bigger than a desire, she knew she would be with someone else, someone who would fall for the woman she had reclaimed – the confident, self-achieving, funny and elegant woman she had grown into through the last three years.

At times there had been self-doubts as she had had to tackle different problems along the way. Both small and large problems would wobble that new self-confidence – the cat dying, sorting out the divorce agreement, ensuring that she was financially OK; she handled it all with dignity even though it was very difficult to do so at times. She knew she had to retain a relationship with her husband for the sake of her son. There were many setbacks – I wouldn't want you to think Sarah's journey was easy and that she didn't have many things which wobbled her. She often questioned whether life would ever be good again.

What Sarah learnt was to listen to her feelings and first of all not be afraid to have a good cry. If she felt like crying then she gave herself permission to do just that and also knew that she could ask for help from her friends and that it was OK to cry with them too

How many times do we women think we can't ask for help, let alone cry with others? For some reason we feel we have to hold it all together.

In the safety of being with a loving friend then it's absolutely fine. If you still doubt what I say, ask yourself how you would react if a close friend cried when talking to you.

You might feel a little uncomfortable, you might not know what to say, you might want to make it all better for her – these reactions are all normal emotions.

All you need to do is to listen and be there for them, allowing them to share with you how they feel and; if you both feel comfortable enough, a hug is also great. Not so good though, is the tendency to do a sticking plaster job – when you want to say 'There, there, it will all be OK tomorrow'. It might not be. Silence is golden in some situations; it is often enough for the person to just be listened to and know that you are there for them.

A simple question is often helpful – 'What could you do about . . .?'

Get them started on the process of considering possibilities and options. If you get an 'I don't know' response, then ask 'What would it be, if you did know?', or 'What would so and so say if you asked them?' or 'What would you say to someone else in this situation?'. Putting the issue into the perspective of someone else is often very helpful.

Sarah got through her difficult times with humour and looking for the good in every situation.

Sarah is still in her forties and travelling down her road of discovery, understanding that success is not a destination but a journey. It helps to know your direction but not necessarily where you will end up, as well as enjoying the journey along the way, making sure you make the most of it.

As her personal confidence grew, Sarah became happier with herself and noticed that she attracted fun and laughter, was able to share good times with others. As a 'people person' who enjoys the company of others and the opposite sex, she was aware that she needed to develop this aspect further. However, not having had a date since her early twenties, this was a very scary thought. How does a forty something meet an eligible man, what does one wear, what do you say, will they find me attractive enough and, oh my God, let's not even think about having sex with a new man.

Sarah began to attract attention from men and it came from the fact that not only was she great to look at, but she was having fun and enjoying herself. The journey she'd been on was enabling her to enjoy her own company again. She realised that she was capable of so much more than she had thought, really giving her a confidence boost. She went and got her hair restyled with a more 'edgy' look and yet still retained her natural elegance. She revamped her look to compliment her great figure, adding colour and panache; she became more youthful and vibrant. She became able to look in the mirror and not only accept herself, but actually think, 'Wow, I look great'. She was able to return to the old days when she had taken time and effort with her looks – for herself, and not considering what anyone else would think.

Because Sarah was balancing her style and vibrant personality well, she grew into a stunning new 'her'.

Where did the inner glow come from? Learning to love herself for who she is, believing in herself, knowing that life is good and she is alive and happy again. Finding happiness in simple pleasures is important; taking each day one at a time and enjoying the moment rather than planning endlessly and over-analysing.

When did you last allow yourself time for simple pleasures and to really savour the moment? It might be enjoying a book and totally absorbing yourself in the story; or having a long leisurely bath with candles and a favourite CD; or taking time to enjoy a really good cup of coffee – especially if you invite a favourite friend too.

Personally a real treat for me is a cappuccino, savouring the whole experience of a full of flavour cup of coffee, and taking some time just for me (away from the kids, my husband and the house). I sometimes just notice the world around me or I love to people watch and wonder what their lives are about – noticing the small intricacies about them. And sometimes I take the time to write, to commit my thoughts and expressions to paper.

Taking just 20 minutes and treating yourself can have a wonderful effect on how you feel. Some of you will enjoy connecting with nature, going for a walk and noticing what's around you – breathing in all the fresh air and elements – refreshing how you feel, increasing your energy levels.

Where have we left Sarah on her current journey? On her vision board was a picture of a woman sitting on a wall in a foreign country just enjoying the moment of being herself and where she was. Sarah had turned into this woman through the journey she had taken. One year she went on holiday with a friend and did indeed find herself sitting on a wall, feeling happy. A gentleman walked by and made conversation, attracted no doubt by the positive feeling she had about herself. They talked and enjoyed each other's company and realised they were on the same excursion, Sarah with her friend and he with his family. That evening they all ended up being seated together and enjoyed the conversation and laughter – although Sarah did notice that his wife didn't join in much and really was rather miserable.

Three months later Sarah received a phone call from the man, John. He explained that he had since left his wife, the holiday had been a last chance to try and work things out, but it hadn't succeeded. He also told Sarah that she had had an amazing impact on him. Talking to her had made him realise that he too wanted to be happy again and feel alive and enjoy life. Over the following months he had taken a brave step and decided to find his own path to future happiness. Was this choice full of difficulties? Yes, and it still is.

Sarah was flattered and surprised by the call. She was also slightly concerned about how he had obtained her number. As their relationship together developed she learnt he had pestered the holiday rep for it, not really knowing whether he would use it but feeling strongly that they might meet again.

So we leave Sarah with John having recently got married, continuing to find happiness together and supporting each other through their still difficult journeys. When she least expected it, love found her. She had faith that it would, and having found a way to love herself for the wonderful woman she was, she was ready to receive it.

Key areas of resilience demonstrated

Self-efficacy

Although Sarah was totally knocked by her husband leaving her, she knew deep down she had it in her to get through this. She pushed herself to do things, building her confidence and belief in her own ability.

Optimism

Sarah does worry, however when she's at her best she is optimistic about the future, believing things will work out and be better than they were. This hope about the future supported her moving forward and trying new things.

Humour

With difficult situations she was able to see the funny side, rather than seeing them as disastrous. Her humour attracted others to her; people enjoy being with those who are uplifting and fun.

Purpose and clarity of direction

Sarah knew she wanted things to change after her husband left her. She didn't know where she wanted to be exactly, but somewhere different.

Visualising through pictures stimulated her thinking and she then set small achievable goals.

Perspective

Getting Sarah to see things through different lenses to her own opened up her overall view. She was able to recognise that her marriage, for the majority of time, had been a good one, rather than letting the recent difficult experience taint it all for her.

Support

Sarah knew she needed the support of her sister and friends and was happy to ask for it. She knew her friends loved her and would be happy to support her. She also learnt to be kinder to herself around what she had achieved and the progress she made.

Reminders for me through writing this chapter

What was powerful to me about Sarah's story was that she recognised through the break up of her marriage that she had lost who she was. As we become close to the people we choose to share our life with we can sometimes distance ourselves from who we are as individuals and what we enjoy. This story reminds me to keep close to who I am as well as what I am.

The other powerful message for me is Sarah's faith and optimism. Yes, it waned and she needed help at times to reconnect with it but she generally believed she would find happiness and love again, and she did.

Strategies to develop resilience Sarah-style

Self-efficacy

Seeing others similar to yourself succeed by sustained effort raises your belief that you possess the capabilities to master activities and succeed. Who do you know and admire that has overcome difficulties, what did they do, how did they feel, how did they succeed? Go and ask them, explore with them what helped them, and copy it, make their ideas and previous experiences your own. Model what others do. Sarah looked at her friends to see what they had done to overcome their difficulties and copied some of what they did. She also saw what hadn't worked and was conscious she didn't want to repeat these particular experiences in her life.

Social persuasion through getting verbal encouragement helps overcome self-doubt and encourages you to give your best effort to the task in hand. Find people who will support you and give you encouragement. Minimise those that don't. Sarah knew which of her friends were right for her at the beginning, who would be gentle, encouraging and patient. Those friends who had different qualities that weren't right at the time she avoided and then picked up with them later when she was ready to do so.

Optimism

Understand that the past does not equal the future. Just because you've experienced pain or disappointment in the past it does not mean that what starts badly will end badly. Do not make a bad start turn into a self-fulfilling prophecy for a bad ending. Sarah had a belief that she would meet someone else, that just because her first marriage didn't last forever it didn't mean that she would never have another loving relationship. Watch for those sweeping statements that generalise everything as being a failure for you. STOP yourself and change your thinking to one of a learning opportunity or recognise that no two situations are ever the same.

Praise people. Notice great things about others and praise them. Take the focus off yourself and generate a sense of positivity. Sarah was always very good at recognising others' strengths and achievements and took time to acknowledge them, both to herself and the individuals concerned. She helped others to recognise their achievements as well as keeping her focus on possibility and accomplishment for herself.

Humour

Challenge yourself to notice the funny side to situations and make a comment about it, if not to others then to yourself. Sarah reconnected with her humour in this way and was able to laugh at her situation.

Purpose and clarity of direction

Create a vision board. Sarah flicked through different magazines to find pictures she liked or felt some connection with and then from this developed her own vision board that we then explored to find the hidden meaning. This gave her more clarity around what she was looking for in her life. If you fancy having some fun creative time then here are the steps to make your vision board.

Buy board or a large piece of card – any colour works. Also buy yourself a box of markers and a glue stick.

Start browsing through magazines and newspapers and cut out images that symbolise your goals and dreams or, as in Sarah's case, just connect with you or that you like. Feel free to download images from the internet as well.

Sometimes words or phrases resonate as much as pictures so cut them out too. This is your vision, you can add what you want. Once you have collected all your images, place them on the board. Feel free to organise the board in THEMES, eg health, romance, career, money, family, etc, or randomly place them where you want. Get creative.

Glue them on to your card and create your vision board.

As you finish, explore what the pictures might mean if you don't know.

The key to your success is that the vision board has to be visible, a place you physically go to it often – your office, your den, your kitchen are all great choices.

Congratulations, you made it, and it's now on your wall. Now, you have to LIVE IT. Visit your vision board frequently. Look at all your pictures, your words. What are you doing to make them come to fruition? But remember, visualisation is just as important as action.

Perspective

Increase your self-awareness, understand who you are, your values, your beliefs, your distinct qualities. What are your goals, both long and short term? When do you say, 'I should do . . .' What are those shoulds and who is it really saying them? Usually when a should appears it's a great clue to us feeling an imposed rule from somewhere or someone. Recognise where the shoulds come from and decide what you really want, not what you think you ought to do. Sarah took time to rediscover who she was, what was important to her and what she wanted in life. That empowered her to move forward with hope and optimism.

Develop your mindfulness, noticing what is going on around you, how you feel, what you see, what you sense, what you hear. Savour the good times and build up a bank of positive experiences you can tap into when needed. Some people anchor these in an object; or a piece of music may be the positive trigger, or a picture. Notice positive experiences, capture them and then place them somewhere so you can reconnect with them, to help lift your mood. If you want to take this a stage further then meditation is also excellent for calming and developing your resilience. Generally you can add mindfulness into your life by noticing the things you see and the experiences you have, rather than rushing. This helps recoup lost energy as well as calming things down, which will enable you to see things differently or more clearly. Sarah started by going for a coffee on her own and being comfortable with herself. This helped her notice the other aspects around her and enabled her to enjoy the journey as well as the end result. Make yourself slow things down and take notice. You might be amazed at what you discover and how it makes you feel, all helping to build your reserves up, as well as helping to open up your mind and perspective on the situation.

Support yourself and others

Allow yourself to be kind to yourself. Stop that negative self-talk. Acknowledge your efforts and achievements openly, initially to yourself and then share them with others; you might even find writing them in a journal empowering. Give yourself some leeway, no one is perfect, we all make mistakes – they are just learning opportunities. Give yourself a treat, take time out, enjoy yourself, make sure you have regular nourishment time, as I call it. It might just be to enjoy a lovely cup of coffee, read a book, ring a friend when you're not in a rush. It doesn't have to be big – although a spa day is wonderful. I've recently discovered cycling and getting out on the mountain bike in the countryside is a great way to reboost me.

Sarah developed the ability to acknowledge her achievements, talking about them and recognising her progress. When she had a setback she learnt how to put it into proportion, ensuring it didn't take over, turning her thoughts to negative ones. How often do you catastrophise a problem, letting it grow and allowing it to consume your thinking and feelings? Stop yourself, detach yourself from it; placing it on a piece of paper so you can look at it from a distance, is sometimes a great place to start.

> *Happiness is not the absence of problems, but the ability to deal with them.* – H Jackson Brown.

Chapter 5

CLARE'S STORY – "DEALING WITH CONSISTENT KNOCK-BACKS"

I met Clare when I was asked to coach each member of the senior management team of a manufacturing site. I had been working with the site manager but he had been promoted to take on a global role and his replacement was an internal promotion from within the senior team. Obviously there were potential issues around the new manager moving from being a peer to line manager; and there were also a few unhealthy behaviours within the team that the old site manager felt, with him leaving, they needed assistance with.

At our first meeting, Clare was very clear about the things that she felt were wrong with the team and her frustrations with the current situation. It was important that I helped Clare understand what she could do and what might be helpful for her to work on through the coaching sessions. You can only influence your own behaviours and actions, not those of others, though the impact of doing so might prompt a different reaction from them.

The senior team was full of emotional outbursts, which had become a way of working that nobody enjoyed, but didn't know how to break or change the pattern. Clare herself realised that she too often responded emotionally when her frustrations built up, especially if she felt she wasn't being listened to or taken seriously. Her initial coaching objectives were to understand people's feelings more and therefore be more sensitive to their needs; to manage her frustration and, in her words, become 'less arsey'; to balance better her whole life, as she felt it was all on top of her and she was struggling to do everything. She also wanted to enhance her communication portfolio so she had more approaches to pull on; she had identified she struggled with certain types of people and wasn't able to influence them effectively.

So what was underneath the frustrations and emotional outbursts and what was happening in other areas of her life that she felt like it was all getting too much? At our initial meeting it struck me with Clare that although on the surface she looked like an individual that 'coped', there was a sense of vulnerability and also a sense of wariness about the coaching process. Clare came across as an outspoken individual who is clear on what needs to be done and how it needs to be done, a straight talker, but on the other hand a person who does listen to others' problems and supports them through their personal difficulties. I wasn't sure though who was looking after Clare.

Over the coming months we did some great work together and Clare really changed; she was no longer frustrated, she learnt how to listen to her feelings sooner and understand what they were telling her and take action earlier. She adapted her style to suit people who were different from her and became more open to differing views and opinions, learning to explore them rather than being quick to dismiss them as they didn't fit with her interpretations. Through this she developed a strong relationship with another member of the senior team with whom it had previously been a little strained. She started to see things from others' perspective and understood others' motivations, enabling her to respond more calmly and improve her influencing ability.

We introduced some fun and relaxation into Clare's life: she was run ragged, was exhausted and feeling like things were beginning to weigh her down. She was the one in the family who seemed to do all the care and support for her mum, often visiting her after a hectic day at work to look after and cook for her, then go home and do the same for her husband and son. I didn't realise at first how significant this was. Two years earlier Clare had had a similar build-up of everything getting on top of her and feeling like everyone was looking to her to deal with it all. She became very low, not knowing how to get out of what seemed like a great bleak black hole.

Something dramatic happened that clicked her out of her despair and she went back into Clare's coping strategy: 'It's down to me so let's get on with it'. After some initial support and assistance from the family she went back to coping mode and, surprise, surprise, the build-up was happening again. Clare's sense of family and responsibility is huge and drives her to take it all on. She is protective of her three brothers and almost mothers them, letting them off; her feeling was that there wasn't really any point in asking them for assistance and listed various reasons on their behalf that meant they couldn't help. We explored what they might be able to do in connection with supporting her mum, generating some ideas that she later shared with them. We discussed 'what did her Mum really need' and was there a difference with what she was offering currently in terms of care and support. This enabled her to move from a visit every evening, to one every other day, and her mum is absolutely fine and doing well. Clare also feels she doesn't have to stick rigidly to the 'every other day' and is able to be more flexible as well as not feel obligated to go.

This opened up discussions about how she could have more fun time with her mum rather than just 'chore' time doing the caring. This was beneficial for Clare in numerous ways; she needed to add more fun into her life and previously had felt too tired to have an enjoyable time with her mum for whom she cared deeply.

Clare had become so independent that she found it difficult to not do the role of looking after everyone else, of being super human.

We were able to extend this approach to her husband. It became clear that Clare had been so tired and distracted with all the chores, workload and stresses that she and her husband had not had any fun time for a while. I remember her being so excited about her wedding anniversary that was approaching; she booked a trip away, just a brief one, where they could relax and spend some fun time, just being together without all the other 'stuff' getting in the way.

Clare began to understand more what she needed and was beginning to accept offers of support and help. She was even beginning to ask her husband and son for support at home to help her balance everything.

This was a real change in behaviour for Clare that didn't come easily as it was different to all her previous strategies for getting through. I think she had a sense that something had to change and here were some simple and safe things that were appearing to work whilst maintaining her identity in the family. Whether it was the previous difficult situation that she knew she didn't want to go back to or whether she just knew that something needed to be different, I don't know.

All this work and progress was extremely significant for Clare in what happened next in her life.

Before I cover that part of her story I think it is really important to go back to her earlier life as a child and young woman to understand more about Clare and the patterns she had developed for herself through life.

We start with Clare age seven. One of her memories of this time is her dad throwing a brick through a bedroom window at her mum, leading to her mother moving out, leaving Clare and her brother. Clare understood why her mum had no option but to move out, it was for her safety. Later in life Clare found out a lot more about how awful it had been for her mum. Her stepfather, Jim, told her how her mum had been abused regularly by her husband. Clare's mother never mentioned it to her children and dealt with it herself: at one stage she lived in a women's support refuge for a period of time but then returned home again.

After moving out Clare's mother still saw her children, but this wasn't without difficulty and danger

Life with dad was not a place for a seven-year-old; he moved in his new woman who had four sons of her own. Clare was expected to wash, clean, cook, etc; her childhood at home had gone in an instant. She also saw things that a seven-year-old shouldn't be subjected to: the four boys that had moved in regularly used to beat up her brother, and being a young girl she wasn't able to do anything to help him. You can understand why Clare is so protective of him as an adult. Life got so bad for her brother that he ran away; this triggered off events that led to Clare and her brother going to live with their mum.

With this they had a sense of childhood again. Clare tells a great little story of how, when living with her dad, she only had two dresses; she had many more when she went to live with her mum and she used to get changed three or four times a day, probably to make sure they were still there. I have an image of this little girl, all floaty in her dresses, probably feeling a little like Cinderella having escaped from the hardship and chores and the environment where others were unkind, to one where she had pretty things and could enjoy dressing up.

After this Clare and her brother said they didn't want to see their father, and this happened less and less.

A very significant man entered Clare's life, her stepfather. You can tell from the way Clare tells you about Jim that he was a special man; after all they had gone through he managed to make the children feel safe, and child like again. Jim and her mum had two sons of their own.. Clare remembers all of them being treated as equal and all as one family. Clare describes early memories of waiting for Jim to come home from the pit; she would sit with him while he ate his tea and chat. This was something she never got from her dad, attention and conversation. She remembers her first holiday when they all went to Skegness, getting £1 a day to spend, and them having so much fun all together. She remembers with fondness Jim's mustard coloured Allegro car which enabled them to all get to Skegness.

Despite the fact that her mum and Jim didn't have much money the house was full of love; they might have had difficulty in the miners' strike being able to get bread and milk, but Clare's memory of this period is full of fondness.

The relationship with Jim became really special. Clare describes him as her best friend, she told him everything, he knew about her troubles, boyfriends, and stories from school. This has carried on through her adult life.

At 18 Clare went to Germany; she was dating at the time and he was posted there with the Army. They worked out the only way Clare would be allowed to join him would be if they got married, so they did.

They were originally going to Germany for six months but ended up stopping for 13 years; she absolutely loved it. It was like an extended family. When the guys were on duty away the wives supported each other and friendships were really strong as the same situation tied them all together. As she says, 'you eat together, work together, shop together, socialise together', really knowing who your friends are. These friends are still important to Clare today. She also managed to develop her career out there finding herself moving from Engine Part Reconciliation to Personnel.

During her time in Germany Clare fell pregnant. She didn't really want a baby, it wasn't something she and Mick had planned, so she did struggle to accept the situation. Now she realises that she is so pleased that she did; her face softens as she smiles, telling you about Conner, who is so important to her.

When Clare left Germany she knew that her marriage was over; she was no longer in love with her husband, it had become more of a friendship. Mick didn't know this as she hadn't yet discussed it with him but, despite having a child with him, she knew it wasn't her future. They arrived back home and moved into a house near to her parents.

She found the courage to discuss how she felt with Mick, which he found difficult to understand and wondered whether she had somebody else, which she hadn't but knew in time she would. To ensure that both of them had a good relationship with Conner, Clare lived in the house in the week and Mick moved in at the weekend while she went to live with a friend. This wasn't really sustainable in the long term and Clare ended up buying a small house for herself and Conner. Clare's stepfather again supported her through this difficulty; interestingly he already had sensed that things weren't right between the couple.

Through work Clare developed a relationship that seemed to be going well. The pair finally managed to go out socially together alone one Sunday and got spotted by the owner of the business. Being the straight talker Clare is and wanting to head things off at the pass she went in on the Monday and spoke to him, to identify where they stood. All was OK and the relationship was allowed to blossom, whilst balancing the professional relationship at work.

Being sensitive, Clare didn't initially introduce Terry to Conner; she wanted to make sure that their relationship had stability in it before this occurred. This was not surprising as she had a real understanding personally about the impact on small children when new figureheads appear in their lives.

All seemed to be going well, her relationship with Terry was getting stronger, she had independence for herself and Conner and she had a job that she enjoyed. Clare describes the next event in her life as 'her world fell apart'. She received a call to say that Jim had died. Clare didn't believe it. Terry wanted to support her and take her to her mum's but Clare just wanted to be on her own. She got in the car and remembers singing the song that was playing on the radio – Ronan Keating's *If Tomorrow Never Comes*.

She got to her mum's and kept saying 'they must have it wrong'. She contacted all her brothers and got them to come home. Then as a family they all went to see her stepfather in the hospital. She stroked his hair and spoke to him and still it didn't really hit her that he had gone. She kicked into her 'it's down to me then' and got everything sorted for the funeral, with her brothers and mum not doing much. She just seemed to know what to do. She was balancing seeing her mother, doing the organising and then being a mum herself. It kept her mind busy.

The day of the funeral came and at first she refused to get into the car, as she knew it was now real and that her emotion, which had been kept at bay through being busy, was bubbling just below the surface and that if she got in the car then that would be it.

For a while afterwards Clare had her stepdad's last message on her answer phone, which gave her some comfort through her loss as she replayed it. She supported others but realised she had lost a great dad and special friend, the person who knew her really well and who she opened up to when she had difficulties in her life.

After the funeral Clare spent lots of time with her mum supporting her but soon realised she couldn't keep it up; being a mum herself and working full time, she had to balance her life and be realistic around what she could continue to do.

Things progressed with Terry and she found herself a new job at the manufacturing site where I met her; life at this time was happy, with holidays together as a family and sometimes with her mum. She married Terry, and had another promotion, responsible for HR on the site, giving her a real challenge but one that she enjoyed.

Just before she got married to Terry, she found a lump on her breast, but didn't tell anybody; she was busy doing the wedding stuff and that took her mind off it. This was the familiar pattern of doing things to keep the emotional aspect at a distance. A couple of months later she watched Gail Porter on television talking about her mum having breast cancer and saying she was considering whether to have a mastectomy as she had a high risk of getting it. This hit home. Clare booked herself in to see the doctor. She quickly got referred to a consultant where she had to have a biopsy; it took two weeks for the results to come back.

At the time this didn't really worry Clare as she had a belief that she would be OK. The results came back and were inconclusive so they had to do a lumpectomy. This lack of confirmation shook Clare and she started to think 'Oh shit!'. Being the protector and carer of others, she didn't initially let her mother know about the situation. Clare was told that there were cells in the lump but that this was OK.

Being a positive individual Clare thought, 'Great, I get a free mammogram every year.'

Clare firmly put this medical issue behind her and got on with her life.

Then two years later her husband found another lump.

Her doctor told her not to worry: she had a mammogram coming up, they would wait for the results. It was clearly visible on the mammogram, a black spot. They got her straight into hospital to see the consultant. She sat in the waiting room on her own. Her husband, she felt, was too emotional to be there. Everything whizzed around in her head: Would it be different to last time or just the same? That black spot didn't look good. What did that mean?

Luckily for Clare she met somebody in the waiting room whom she had known through her time in Germany. Talking to Pam about what had been happening to her helped her take the focus off her mind fantasising.

Making conversation with others is a way that helps Clare through difficulties. She had previously always gone to her step dad and talked things through with him; having that objective support without too much emotion really helped Clare deal with things. The same medical process as before took place. Clare had to wait again for two weeks for the biopsy results; this time she was more tense, although still optimistic. When she went to get the results, she knew it was not good news. The consultant held Clare's hand and spoke to her in medical jargon which, as she was emotionally all over the place expecting the worst, she probably wouldn't have heard whatever he had said. When he had finished Clare, in her straightforward, way asked him, 'Am I going to die?' The consultant reassured her that she wasn't. 'I'm OK with that,' was Clare's response.

Clare's approach to adversity had always been, OK stiff upper lip, let's get on with, whatever I need to do. Initially it was the same this time. She sat with the nurse who talked her through the next steps and what was likely to happen at each stage. Clare got into her car, had a few minutes to herself to reflect and consider what she had just been told, and then kicked herself back into action.

She was driving back to work and thought she probably needed to tell Terry, so detoured to see him at work. They sat in the car together and she told him that she would be fine but would need further treatment and talked him through the situation.

Grabbing at normality Clare went back to work; there were a number of people who knew her well enough to know that things weren't good just by looking at her.

Her boss, after a discussion with Clare, decided that it would be helpful for her managerial peers to know about her situation. This was definitely unfamiliar ground for Clare as normally she would have just carried on with hardly anybody knowing and her really not wanting any difficulty acknowledged or sympathy given. She was with her boss when they told her peers and the reaction was something she hadn't expected. One cried; another was stunned into silence. Typical Clare with her humour, said that one of her male colleagues then became fixed on her chest and her quick retort to this was, 'It's still there, it's still the same!' Making a joke of it eased the situation for them and her. They were all extremely supportive and wanted to know what she wanted from them to help. She explained that she needed normality, to be able to come to work and do what was required of her, but she knew realistically she wasn't going to be able to be as effective or productive as she was normally, so could they really think about what they needed her for and when she asked would they take on work on her behalf. Asking for support was not what Clare did but she realised she needed to; she had worked on being more open in her relationships with others which created a platform now for her to try a different approach in these difficult times.

This morning I spent 40 minutes on the bike in the gym; the instructor had been honest with me about what I needed to do to achieve the goals I wanted.. Didn't really want to hear it, let alone do it: increase my cardiovascular work to 40/45 minutes at least three times a week. The exercises I had been doing weren't really doing much so he gave me a few different ones that worked all my body. Why share this in the middle of Clare's story? Well it struck me that resilience shows itself at different levels, intensity and in different situations and we don't really notice it. So despite aching from working at the weekend in the gym, I got on the bike, headphones on, head down and off. OK for the first 15 minutes; this is when I would normally think it's now getting a bit difficult, my bum hurts, the legs ache and sweating too much, time to get off. Managed to get over that hurdle, so to speak, and carry on. I was listening to the radio and the DJ was being rather funny so that helped take my mind off it for a bit. An older gentleman, who I know to be in his seventies, cycled opposite me and made my efforts look a bit weak. I didn't let that put me off, I cycled on through the pain. I thought about my husband who is training for a cycle ride for charity; he is a member of a team of four and they have to cycle for 24 hours, taking turns on the bike, an hour at a time. In the middle of the night you're on the bike doing your stint, the supporters have gone, you ache from previous sessions. How on earth will he do it? What keeps him going? I can't get the energy and motivation to do the 40 minutes suggested by the gym instructor. Thinking about this while cycling myself made me have even more admiration for my husband and got me focused on my end goal . . . just ten minutes to go.

I thought about the characteristics that help my husband with this training, as I have no doubt that he will be successful in the event. He has a clear sense of purpose, knowing what and why he wants to achieve it, he has small goals, milestones to measure his success by and show him he is heading in the right direction. We have all used humour – have you seen the outfits they wear for professional cycling, if you've not got a sense of humour I'm not sure you'd wear the gear. My husband knows he will achieve this goal, there is no waver and before he started he had not been on his racing bike for over 20 years. He has read magazines and training material to ensure he takes on board others' views and ideas and adapts them to fit his requirements. The weather has scuppered his plans a little as it has rained and rained and rained this year. So being flexible he spoke to a friend who does triathlons and now has some contraption attached to the bike in the garage so he can train on the spot so to speak. The family have given him support through encouragement, time, diet and being flexible around his need to go off and do the training. He has shown great resilience within this challenge he has set himself – others may give up or don't do the training so aren't able to compete to their best.

This helped me push through the last few minutes on the exercise bike, thinking about his qualities and how resilience shows itself through many things we do. I did finish my 40 minutes, felt like cheering, not really what you do in a gym, but I did in my head, wobbled off the bike and thought I know this is nowhere near as challenging as what my husband is tackling but for me this morning I do feel I've pushed beyond what I would normally do and feel better for it, well psychologically. I texted him to let him know my achievement and sent a message of admiration for him with his challenge. I got a lovely message of support back which really gave me a boost; others recognising where you have pushed yourself or doing something you wouldn't normally do, really gives you that extra encouragement that helps you through difficult times. Although I wasn't looking for support, this is what I got and it really made the cycle even more worthwhile. I shall hold on to all these thoughts when I do my next 40 minutes.

Clare held onto the support she was given through her cancer; it makes her emotional, which is not a trait you would naturally put with her. She tells you about people she didn't expect to offer her support, the kind words that people gave her and the acts of unconditional kindness. The factory workers that she supports in her HR role are generally men who don't do feelings and have previously given her a hard time re negotiations with the unions, etc. But she received nice words in cards, advice from some who had had family members with a similar illness. People told her how much they admired her bravery with it all and her positive approach.

After her lumpectomy operation Clare, being one for limited fuss and getting back to normal, came home on the same day; Terry drove her. She felt sick and awful but wasn't sharing it otherwise she knew her husband would have her straight back in the hospital and she knew that this wasn't the right place for her, she wanted to be back at home. She was so tired and in pain but sat and convalesced, well for a few days.

Clare then went back to work while she waited to find out what treatment was still required. Waiting is not something that Clare finds easy so distractions are what help her through.

Treatment could be in different forms: Herceptin, chemotherapy, radiotherapy. The nurse who was supporting Clare came to the house and talked her and her family through the next stages in the treatment, she even brought a special book for her teenage son and ensured he knew how to get hold of her if he had any questions or needed some support himself. Clare describes her nurse, Jill, with fondness and as a woman who has a calling rather than someone who is just working. Which is no doubt why she was so special in her approach and in the care she offered to Clare and her family throughout this time.

The recommendation for Clare was to have chemotherapy and then radiotherapy; you can't be forced to have chemotherapy and some women do refuse to have it for vanity reasons. Chemotherapy affects the whole of the body and is more preventative where as radiotherapy targets the spot where the cancer is. Clare considered her options and spoke to the doctor, her family, and the nurse and decided that she was going to have chemotherapy. It began six weeks after the operation. Chemo starts to dominate your life; the day before the treatment you have to go to hospital so they can check your bloods; this really didn't take long but the waiting around seemed to take ages. Then the following day, there's a full day in the hospital. This goes on for 18 weeks where every three weeks you have to follow this routine, unless you are unlucky and your bloods aren't right and you get put back a week; luckily this only happened once to Clare.

During treatment Clare had to sit in a chair, with a drip in, for four hours — this is a woman who is active and normally deals with things through doing, but she was constrained to a chair. What did she do to help her?

She spent her time phoning, texting, catching up on emails for work and reading magazines. But what really helped Clare was her ability to connect with others and have a laugh with those around her in the same situation.

After her first treatment she felt OK and other than the taste of metal in her mouth, she felt no different. This was what happened after the second treatment; she was beginning to think that it wasn't too bad and she was lucky that she didn't feel worse and then . . . She was drying her hair one morning and her fringe fell out in her hand.

I know personally this would hit me hard. Every time I move house the two most stressful things for me are finding a dentist and a hairdresser. If my hair isn't right I don't feel right. I can't imagine how I would have been with a hand full of hair from my fringe and looking at a large gap on my head. Despite the fact that you know this might happen, preparing for it occurring, well I don't think you can.

Clare had already got a wig ready for when this might happen; she hadn't known when or how it would happen, slowly or in clumps. How was she going to cope? Being Clare it was all about dealing with it practically.

She rang her hairdresser who was a friend and asked if she could squeeze her in for a trim. She sat in the chair and asked her friend to take it all off. Her friend sobbed all the way through cutting Clare's hair. Clare turned to humour as she often does in difficult situations and said, 'You know, I've been coming to you for all these years to have my hair done, as it's falling out, can I have all my money back?' – trying to make light of the situation.

When she went home, Terry, her husband, couldn't believe that she'd been and done it. As with a lot of things, once she's made her mind up Clare gets on and does it. This was another of those situations, no point in taking days to consider what to do when she knew it would just get worse; make the decision and execute it. She had bought scarves and she did wear her wig twice. One day she didn't realise she didn't have it on. She had competed in Race for Life with no wig or scarf and then on the way home went to the supermarket and a small boy said to his mum, 'She's got no hair. She's like granddad.' The parents were embarrassed and hushed up the child. Children are great, they approach life in a very simple way, speaking their thoughts out loud, which often makes the issue easier to deal with as it's out there on the table, so to speak. Clare had a little giggle to herself and smiled at the child and went about her shopping.

For some this would have been embarrassing, or another reminder of their illness, and knocked them back, but for Clare it was the turning point to be who she was at this moment in time and not wear anything on her head. Lots of other women used to say to her, 'I don't know how you do it.' Her reply usually was one of humour, 'bald is beautiful, it's the new look.'

She felt less conscious without anything on her head and, in her words, just got on with it.

Clare was still confident in how she looked and felt despite not conforming to the norm of having a full head of hair. This level of confidence and simplistic approach to the situation was one of action and moving forward, not dwelling on the emotion. Whenever she was taking action she felt she had an element of control and was able move her life forward through the illness.

Her loss of hair also provided an opportunity of intimacy for her and Terry; he used to shave her head for her and was really gentle. They would talk, he would massage lotion onto her head after he had shaved it. It became their special time, a time when Terry was needed and was able to care for Clare and one where Clare was able to enjoy being close with the man she loved while sharing together what was happening to her.

Throughout her treatment Clare developed some friendships and found comradeship with people who were experiencing the same situation as herself. She was conscious of the emotions and feelings of those close to her and what was great for her was that when at the hospital she didn't have to think about this; she could just be herself with others who were dealing with the same stuff. So when the treatment came to an end she had mixed emotions. It was great that this part was over, but on the other hand she knew she would miss the connection with the people who had been through everything with her. Clare felt quite sad, but grateful as she knew the conversations had helped her through the difficult afternoons having the treatment.

The experience has really helped her understand what real friendship is. There were people who she thought were friends who didn't show any element of empathy and understanding to her situation, that didn't offer any support. In contrast others she knew, who she wouldn't necessarily describe as friends, seemed to understand her and instinctively offered her what she needed, giving freely of their time and effort to support Clare.

Throughout the treatment Clare continued to work. This time she was sensible and knew when she needed to go home and rest, but it became her constant support and purpose that helped her through those challenging times. She mentioned that the treatment and the illness can be totally absorbing. You spend hours around others with cancer, in the hospital, with yourself and family at home; if you're not careful it will consume you. Which Clare didn't want, she knew that work would take her mind off it, remind her that she had a life and she was working towards being well rather then being ill. Mentally she was fine and working enabled her to use her brain and show herself that she was still capable of doing something that she enjoyed, and was needed by others.

Clare felt she was selfish through her treatment; she needed to work and she needed to deal with aspects of her situation, rather than be concerned about others. I don't see this as selfish, I see this as being brave, assertive and clear about what she knew she needed to help her get through this. We often, especially in times of upset, let others take control and this is probably great in the short term while you come to terms with something, but it hands over the responsibility to someone else, and you may become resentful or blaming when they don't give you what you need. Clare knew herself well enough to know what she needed and she explained this to the ones she cared about so they understood it wasn't her rebuffing their love and support, it was about giving her support in a different way that suited her.

I remember one day when I was having a catch up with Clare through the treatment she telling me about how she knew she'd made great progress with accepting support in connection with allowing others to do things for her. Her husband had been doing the housework, which was not the norm. She had sat in the lounge watching, probably not a good idea, however she was so pleased with herself as she had not picked fault with the way he was doing the cleaning, despite the fact that he wasn't doing it right! She had worked exceptionally hard to manage herself and not criticise or nit pick; she had even got to the stage where she thanked and complimented him. She was always someone who pointed out what was missing or what else needed doing, generally in a helpful way, though others didn't always receive it that way. So restraining herself, I knew, was a massive leap forward for her.

Dealing with a teenage son during difficult times also requires sensitive thinking, enabling him to talk and air his concerns rather than him thinking that he mustn't burden his mum. Clare managed this and Conner, her son, aired his biggest fear. Was she going to die? As Clare was confident about this, as she had asked the consultant, she was able to deliver her response with conviction and belief, which enabled Conner to believe it too. There was no question in Clare's mind: she would get over and be rid of the cancer so she could continue to lead her life how she wanted. This reassurance no doubt gave her son the confidence to deal with the changes he saw in his mum as she was often ill after treatment.

Conner was a key driver in Clare having the strength and positive approach to the cancer. She was clear she wanted to see Conner grow into a man and be able to share his future life with him. The love for him gave her strength and stopped her feeling sorry for herself for long. She did dip and found aspects difficult but being able to connect to something that was important in her life enabled her to shake off those feelings and 'get on with it'.

After the chemotherapy came the radiotherapy. Every day for seven or so weeks she had to go to hospital, which for Clare was a long trip as she didn't live nearby. She still managed to fit in work, going in the morning, then travelling to the hospital, and then returning home, as you can imagine, rather shattered. This became her new routine and she met new people and continued to maintain a humorous approach to it all. For nearly a year her life revolved round hospital visits. It was consuming and tiring, but she managed to approach it all with an upbeat manner. Knowing it was her route to getting healthy again, she just did what she needed to do.

At last Clare's treatment finished.

Her husband who, Clare said, never plans surprises, did. He walked in the house just after she arrived home from the last treatment with a large bouquet of flowers, told her to get changed, they were going out. He treated her to a lovely meal; they knew they were celebrating their future life together which was so much more significant than it had been the previous time they'd been out to celebrate together on their last wedding anniversary.

Clare walked into work the next day thinking it would be no different, other than that she was there for the full day, rather than having to dash off to the hospital. Her office was full of congratulations banners, flowers, cards and balloons. This overwhelmed her and she broke down and sobbed, probably feeling the relief herself of what she been through as well as the overwhelming love she felt from her work colleagues and friends who had helped get her through the ordeal.

During the year she had noticed her son struggling emotionally, often a bit withdrawn even though she ensured there were opportunities for him to be able to talk. She just put it down to him having to deal with his mum having cancer. After her treatment, Conner decided to open up a little more about what was on his mind. He had also been understanding more about himself during the year and was clear that he was gay. It had not felt right to talk to Clare during her illness but now her worries were over he was able to. Because they had developed a really strong relationship as he grew into a teenager and through her illness they were able to talk about this in a balanced and supportive way, where he felt safe and able to be who he was.

Conner had probably seen his mum being strong to who she was through the last year and it had no doubt given him the courage to listen to his emotions and feelings and understand who he was and be prepared to share that with others. Clare didn't realise that she was being a great role model to her son, giving him confidence to be true to himself and talk to others about his needs.

You would think everything that had happened was enough for one year, however it wasn't. During her treatment Clare was also dealing with difficulties at work. I started this story by briefly mentioning that the senior team at the manufacturing site were demonstrating some unhealthy behaviours and having one of the team, Paul, promoted to be their new manager definitely created massive tension, especially for Clare. As equals they had a fiery relationship that was also supportive. But often colleagues would be uncomfortable with the expressive nature in which they would air their differences; some were unsure how to read it, felt it inappropriate, especially in team meetings, and were generally concerned about it continuing now Paul was site manager. Paul and Clare had got into a habit: if they disagreed, pretty much a full scale argument occurred. Clare had supported Paul in his previous role and they had worked closely on some difficult issues. Paul had enjoyed their 'sparring' but recognised that this wasn't going to be the right relationship for his new position, but breaking a habit is difficult and he was also aware that Clare knew him well and that made him feel a little vulnerable.

Paul wanted to assert his new position. He genuinely believed it would be better if Clare was in an office by herself so moved her out of the space she shared with her team into the office next door to his. This sounds simple and if handled in the right way would have been. The discussion was clumsy and the result was that Clare felt 'done to', that he was being aggressive, not really giving her a clear explanation as to his reasons or helping her to understand why she was having to move.

Throughout this time Clare received real mixed messages from Paul – one of being exceptionally supportive re her cancer and the other this controlling aggressive approach whenever she challenged his thinking or ideas. Clare also felt split loyalties as she had become fond of Paul in their time together and really wanted him to work out as the site manager but struggled with the impact on her personally.

To help her deal with this difficult situation she developed a more distant approach, one where she was trying to manage the emotional impact on herself. This was extremely difficult and she didn't always succeed but she made great progress, presenting information in a professional manner without the emotion. Managing her emotion was the biggest challenge, but did it make a difference when she mastered it? Absolutely. She felt less drained, felt that she had maintained her professionalism and that criticism couldn't be thrown back at her as a defence mechanism.

Getting her to see the other side of the situation, a different perspective on some of the things that were going on at work, was helpful in trying to understand Paul's vulnerabilities and approach.

However there was one issue that kept raising its head, one that Clare was having difficulty not focusing on. Clare and a few others in the senior site team thought Paul's relationship with another member of the team was more than just a professional. This impacted on the trust between them, the way people behaved, and was working against any attempts to build a team.

Clare confronted Paul. You might think she should have minded her own business, or you might think she was brave to raise the issue directly with him, but Clare's motivations were to try and get Paul to see what was happening and try and rescue the situation. Her loyalty to him was still there. Also as a HR manager you have a sense of responsibility to give feedback to senior staff about their behaviour if it is negatively impacting on the performance of others.

Oh how much simpler life would have been if Paul had acknowledged the situation to Clare there and then and they could have worked together on a solution. But he didn't. He continued to deny the relationship between him and an other member of the team.

Clare found herself in a difficult position where she found some potential irregularities that she knew she would have to report higher up the line.

Clare had a mix of emotions, around the situation she found herself in, anger, upset that she had been the one that had found it; she felt like she had betrayed a friend who had supported her through her cancer treatment. But there was also a sense that he had used her and tried to manipulate her, that he had turned into somebody during this last year that he wasn't really like and that's why he had been so awful.

For most of us this situation would have been difficult to handle. Clare took a brave step in reporting her friend and colleague. All this was on top of her dealing with her cancer treatment.

Clare has grown so much over the time I have been lucky enough to work with her. She is so much more balanced, she has more equal relationships through allowing others to support her, rather than always being the one to look after everyone else, and she is able to understand what she needs more and work out how to get what she needs.

Which is where we leave her, working on what she needs and wants for the next stage in her career. There has been a restructure at work and Clare has a bigger challenge which I have no doubt she will tackle with professionalism and energy. However, she is reconnecting with what she wants and is deciding if this is the long term direction for her. Great. It would have been easy for Clare to say, 'After the year I've had I just want some time out and carry on as I am,' but she now understands that you have choices, you have to consider them and make the right ones happen for you.

Key areas of resilience demonstrated

Self-efficacy

Clare has developed through her life a strong understanding of who she is and that she is able to deal with difficulties. She takes action, takes control and moves things on she ultimately knows she can deal with. Her self-confidence was demonstrated in the way in which she decided to deal with her hair falling out. 'Shave it off. I am who I am. I don't need wigs and scarves.'

Humour

When things became emotional for people around her then she often used humour to lighten the mood and lift others. She tells stories in a way that makes others smile, despite the fact they may be difficult. She uses humour to help herself and others and lifts the mood.

Emotional self-control

Clare learnt to understand her emotions and what triggered them. She then developed her emotional response from being reactionary to one where she was in control and considered in her approach. This became a powerful tool both in her personal and work life and she admits is still a work in progress.

Purpose and clarity of direction

Through her cancer treatment, she was clear she was going to be well again, as she wanted to be able to share a long life with her son. This drove her motivation, knowing the bigger reason why getting fit and healthy was ultimately important.

The other aspect she demonstrated was ensuring she took action, small steps moving forward to get herself well. She didn't dwell on things or not make decisions, she made them and moved on, giving her a sense of control.

Support

Support is an area that has been a challenge to Clare as often she took the view 'well it's down to me'. However, she learnt the power of connection with others and allowing them to support. She recognised not only how it helped her but helped them; people wanted to offer support and help. Previously her high independence had pushed people away.

She had always supported others and gained a lot from it personally, but has learnt the ability to stand back and allow others to take responsibility rather than doing everything herself.

Reminders for me through writing this chapter

Being a little similar to Clare, in the fact that I too can sometimes take the 'well it's down to me then' approach, it has reminded me that letting others in to support you is powerful for both parties. Human nature is generally one where we want to help others and not allowing others to do so is not helpful in building stronger relationships.

Clare was clear on what kind of help/support would be right for her. So let others know how they can help to ensure you still feel in control and supported in a way that's right for you.

There was also her bravery to do what's right, how she dealt with the difficult issue at work, as well as how she dealt with her cancer. Are we brave enough in our lives? Do we take the 'safe' route too often? Be brave more often.

Strategies to develop resilience Clare-style

Self-efficacy

Developing short term specific goals that will challenge, but are attainable. Clare was constantly moving forward and taking action. So think, what 'can' you do to take action, move forward? What are the next steps for you? Make the decision and then do them. This will develop your confidence in your capability that you can do things and are capable of moving forward.

Understand yourself well, know how to use your skills, knowledge and strengths to help you. Learn who you are and what you are capable of. Take time to consider what's got you to where you are now? What skills, talents and strengths have you shown in previous situations? Recognising what you have done enables you to tap into those skills again in the future. We often think we don't have any, however we all have a number of skills and talents that got us to where we are today. Make a list of what yours are and evidence them through linking them to previous situations. If you're not feeling resourceful then get the list out and remind yourself what you have.

Challenge your negative assumptions, create a different perception of your present reality. We all make assumptions about situations and people. Acknowledge what they are. Ask yourself,

'What assumptions am I making about this?'

'Which of those assumptions is most stopping you moving forward?'

Nancy Kline has a great technique in her Time to Think process (see her book *Time to Think*) that really gets you to challenge your assumptions. Once you've identified which assumption is most stopping you, ask yourself this:

'Given that the assumption is stopping you from moving forward, what could you credibly assume instead?'

Then ask,

'If you knew this new freeing assumption . . . to be true, how would you move forward?'

As a trained 'Thinking Partner' myself, exploring assumptions can be extremely powerful, as we often don't acknowledge what we are assuming. Once we do we can explore what impact they are having on preventing us moving forward, or which positive assumptions we wish to carry forward with us to help us.

Take time to recognise your successes and achievements. We have all had successes and achievements, but we often skip over them and don't acknowledge them. Taking time to recognise them will help you build your self-efficacy, remembering what you have done, what you are capable of. Take some time out and really consider what you have done, note it down so you can reflect on it when you need to give yourself a boost.

Humour

Learn to laugh at yourself and the situations you find yourself in. Clare often found the funny side of life, and sharing this out loud with others enabled her and others to laugh at what was happening. Through lightening the mood of the event we lessen the significance of it as well as giving ourselves a boost through laughing.

Learn to not take life so seriously. When you go through something serious it enables you to have a different perspective on life as other things don't seem as significant as they did before. In Clare's case, the cancer was a very sobering situation. We don't need something so serious to help us consider things in a less serious manner. What's the worst that can happen around this situation? What's the best that can happen? and What's most likely to happen? – just asking ourselves these questions can help change our perspective.

Clare had lost the importance of fun. Schedule time to have fun downtime, doing something that you enjoy with people that make you feel good. Make time for it and plan it in. If you feel a bit more adventurous then plan some new exciting activity that you know will make you laugh, or just simply spend time with people who you know will lift you.

Emotional self-control

For Clare this was extremely difficult, she was a very expressive individual and her thoughts and feelings were often displayed openly. At times this was not helpful, it created explosive, defensive or just difficult conversations with others.

Start to gauge how you are feeling and notice the signals so you begin to understand earlier your feelings and what they mean. Learn to spot the negative feelings and emotions creeping up on you sooner, and determine what to do to change them, rather than just react to them.

Understand what your triggers are, be aware of what situations are most likely to evoke an emotional outburst from you, learn to spot them early and plan for when they might occur.

I had a client that learnt that as a potential emotional outburst was brewing, which generally occurred quickly, the back of her neck became hot. This was her trigger, which once she knew it she could act upon that to prevent the outburst.

Practise being non-judgmental; often emotional charges are stimulated by us being judgmental about others. Learn to accept others for who and what they are. 'Be curious, not judgmental' – Walt Whitman. Take time to understand the other person's view and thinking, ask lots of questions to learn more. Recognise and accept that others will do things differently to you, your way is right for you but it may not be right for others. Check yourself and notice when you are being judgmental about others, challenge yourself to stop and explore, to find out more and accept who they are.

Purpose and clarity of direction

Take time to explore your personal values, the rules by which you live your life, the things that are truly important to you. Understanding what these are enables you to better understand the decisions that you make and the direction of travel that would give you greater fulfillment. Clare was clear that Conner was the most important thing in her life and she wanted to ensure she took his thoughts and views into consideration when she was ill and made time for him to explore his feelings and concerns.

At work she also knew that despite her relationship with Paul, he had crossed her values and she knew she had to raise the matter with her boss. Having this clear sense of what was right and wrong, and what's important, gave her direction and made decisions easier for her.

It's important to us to have our personal values fulfilled. Sometimes we may find ourselves not aligned to organisations that we work within but don't understand why. It's usually linked to the fact that they do things that grate against our personal values. So knowing what they are helps you understand what you need.

To help you identify what they might be, ask the following:

- What's really important to you in your life?
- What does that give you?
- What else is important to you in your life?
- What does that bring you?
- What do you enjoy doing?
- What does that give you/bring you?
- What annoys you? What gets under your skin?
- If XYZ annoys you then what is the positive opposite? What is it that is important to you?

Another way to explore your values is to identify times when you were happiest and what was it that you were doing and what made it happy for you.

When were you most proud and what were the reasons for you being proud?

When have you felt most fulfilled and satisfied, what need or desire was fulfilled.

Once you know your values, you can check that all future goals support your values, giving you a strong connection to them, compelling you to move forward with them. This gave Clare that extra motivation to move forward through her illness, knowing she wanted to spend as much time in her future life, sharing it with her son.

Support

Taking time to support others is a great way to develop your resilience. It distracts you from your issues and helps you see others less fortunate. It also makes you genuinely feel good, having given someone else some support, advice, assistance. Again, it doesn't have to be big gestures – just helping someone cross the road, doing their shopping. If this really appeals then take time in your life to really support others by getting involved in something that is important to you. It might be volunteering, it might be helping someone near where you live, it might be helping a child to read. Find what it is and get involved, see how it nourishes you. There has been lots of research in the world of positive psychology around the long term benefits of random acts of kindness – not planned, but genuine help to others as you see the opportunity – in how they can boost your mood. Take time to notice others and see where you may go with your random acts of kindness.

It was important to get Clare to understand her previous patterns around support and that her previous habits may not be the most helpful for her. Once she realised what she did and was clear about the impact it was having on her general health and happiness she was able to plan an alternative route. We have a tendency to operate as we always have; understanding what our habits are is the first step to changing them. You then need to replace the pattern with a new one otherwise you will just revert back to what you've always done. Changing a habit takes time over a consistent period of time with you consciously being aware of the new behaviour you want to embed to become the habit. Work at it consciously until you find yourself automatically doing the new behaviour.

Humour is just another defence against the universe. – Mel Brooks.

103

Chapter 6

SARAH CRESSELL'S STORY – "THE POWER OF PASSION AND GOAL SETTING"

I met Sarah by chance at an extraordinary women's event. She had kindly paid me a compliment; I was wearing a rather eye catching pair of deep pink leopard skin shoes which had grabbed Sarah's attention.

We got chatting about what had brought her to the event and I soon found out that she had been short-listed to the final three in one of the categories. Being the inquisitive individual that I am, I asked lots of questions about her life and what had brought her to being an entry for this event. Her story was one that fascinated me even in the brief discussion we had. Here was a woman who, despite many setbacks, found herself running a very successful franchise business which fitted around her being a mother.

I took the plunge and asked if she would mind me contacting her to find out more abut her story and whether she would be interested in appearing in my book.

Luckily she agreed and having found out more about Sarah and her journey I am so pleased she did. Her story is a great inspiration for all women about what can be achieved through personal challenges and goal setting.

Sarah told me about her childhood: she is the youngest of six children and she remembers that there was never enough chocolate in the house for her liking. Her dad died when she was eight and her mum worked hard to raise them all. Chocolate became even more scarce in the household and realising that there was no golden ticket like in *Charlie and the Chocolate Factory* to bring her all that she wanted, Sarah, an imaginative child, wrote a comic. The story was all about a fancy dress party and aliens that had come down to Earth. They joined the party but as it was a fancy dress party so nobody spotted them. They zapped everybody and took them back to their planet, asking for a huge ransom of chocolate for them to be returned. As the driver for this creativity was all about having more chocolate she sent the comic to Mars and received a large box of chocolates in return.

Inspired by this success she developed the idea further by selling a 'read' of her comic to her class mates for 1p a go. Sounded like a plan, however on this occasion Sarah didn't gain more chocolate, the comic got ripped and she wasn't really any good at collecting the money. An early lesson in trading that has no doubt assisted her in life when she began to run her own business.

Not one to give up, Sarah was inspired to take a different approach when she noticed the unusual and exciting pencil case of a girl in her class. Rather than having the normal pens and pencils it was overflowing with sweets. She discovered that this girl's parents owned a sweet shop – who needed *Charlie and the Chocolate Factory*'s golden ticket when she knew somebody with an endless supply of sweets? Being the entrepreneur, even at this early stage, she decided to trade her comic 'read' for sweets. Because this *gave* her what she wanted, she *didn't* forget to collect the sweets in return for the read.

This creative element continued as a child and she spent hours in the shed making things, papier-mâché models, pots, escaping into her imaginary world. Sarah didn't sell these, she gave them away as presents, or visitors to the shed got a free spoonful of runny fudge.

Often in our childhood we find ourselves doing what we are naturally talented to do. As well as really enjoying it, you will see from Sarah's story that she ends up back there tapping into those early creative talents.

Having a mum with a practical approach to life Sarah was encouraged to do a degree in catering. Her mum said 'people need to eat' so it seemed like a good idea for a career.

Maybe another of life's early messages was about where she *didn't* want to end up. Whilst looking at Huddersfield Poly, and not having a great sense of direction, she found herself at the counter of the dole office, but only asking for help for which way to go on this occasion.

Sarah ended up at Huddersfield University doing catering. This didn't go as smoothly as she had hoped – while she was there her brother died unexpectedly, which caused her to rethink.

Six weeks after losing her brother she left to work on a kibbutz in Israel. It had been the possibility of adventure, exploration and being able to discover a new part of the world that had drawn her to getting a place on the kibbutz. She struggled emotionally to begin with between what she wanted to do, the loss of her brother and not having her mum nearby but she knew instinctively that this was where she needed to be. She remembers one day sitting on the back of a truck thinking about her brother, Paul, the wind was flying through her hair and the sun warming her body, at the same time listening to *Wonderful Life* by Black. She thought to herself, 'You just have to find the way to make it wonderful.'

Sarah's early philosophy no doubt gave her the ability to find the positive in difficult situations, and to look at things through different eyes. It shows how you, anyone, can make life wonderful for yourself and the others you love, despite the difficulties you have to deal with.

Songs can often give us inspiration and new thinking.

Sarah travelled a lot during her time in Huddersfield . She also went back to her early interests of painting and making things, often giving away her work as gifts as she had done as a child. It wasn't until her last year that she sold her first piece. It felt fabulous to have it recognised by somebody else as being good enough to receive money for it.

Around this time Bob Geldof was in Africa raising awareness about the famine – Live Aid being a big event that featured in most people's lives. She felt pulled to do something about this and, being someone who often listened to her instincts, wanted to find a way to be able to get there. Her sister had applied but had not been successful at getting onto Operation Raleigh, and this gave her an idea of how she might achieve her next goal.

Having the philosophy 'if it's meant to be, it's meant to be' she initially did nothing to help her chances of getting on the trip. She then thought, 'What if I do everything in my power to help me get on the trip, what might that be like? Would it help my chances? Would it make me feel I was doing something towards achieving it and how might that feel?' With this new focus she got up every morning to go running; being fit for the trip was going to be vital. In this respect she had assumed she would be successful and was thinking beyond the getting accepted to what was required of her when on the trip, the need to be fit. She also fully researched all she could about it, mentally focusing positively on achieving this goal.

Well she was successful and once accepted she had to raise £1,500. So Sarah went back to her creativity to make money – designing and printing T-shirts. At one stage she had paid out £750 to buy materials and had not earned a penny, but she had confidence in her ability, that her products were good and that they would sell.

Having this belief in yourself enables you to carry on and move forward. Knowing that she had the ability to achieve success powered her forward. To add to the T-shirts Sarah bought lots of chocolate – a regular theme here – and went round the pubs in Covent Garden selling it.

This part wasn't something Sarah enjoyed, finding it really hard and having no moral support from friends (her friends weren't around her at this time). But she pushed herself to sell despite not wanting to. Focusing on the end goal, of being able to get to Africa, was something that got her through this.

When the day arrived for Sarah to leave for Africa – the dream she had been working towards – how was she feeling? Excited, happy? No, she was scared, she kept being sick, her stomach was churning, she felt wobbly and apprehensive. She suddenly realised that she didn't know anybody else who was going, she had no idea how long she would be out there. To make matters worse the plane was delayed so the feeling seemed to just build while she sat there waiting in the airport. But Sarah didn't run, or change her mind, despite feeling afraid.

Looking back on this she realised this had taught her a great lesson – that often fear of the unknown is worse than the reality. We tend to build things up out of all perspective with our imagination creating big scary pictures of what something's going to be like. Being aware of this then enables you to deal with those emotions more rationally, helping to overcome them.

Sarah spent ten awesome months in Africa and made some incredible friends, not surprisingly using her practical catering skills to ensure everybody was fed. Sarah also found herself using her creative skills – giving the camp that extra special touch with sculptures and decorations – and this got her talents noticed.

She was asked to set up and run a women's art and craft co-operative rural business development centre. As Sarah said, this was absolutely her perfect job. Somebody had spotted the talent that Sarah couldn't help herself from doing wherever she was in the world. And her entrepreneurial acumen was needed as well as her creativity.

This opportunity definitely gave her a great grounding in where she wanted to take her life in the future, setting up her own business, as well as understanding her need to be creative in whatever she did.

Sarah remembers being told by her mum, when she was young, 'to aim high'. This gave her a total belief that anything was possible. She reminded herself of this when she was deciding whether or not to set up her own business. Her early childhood grounding also taught her that she was responsible for the future she created, it was down to her and she had to stand on her own two feet to make things happen – just as it had been when she was a child trying to get more chocolate.

Sarah has developed her own beliefs as she has grown with an ethos that you should take responsibility for what you do, give something back to your community and never do anything you aren't proud of. This is what she uses to guide herself forward through life now. These are like Sarah's rules by which she lives. I often work with individuals to help them identify their rules or, as we call them in the coaching world, their values, by which they live. They are often unspoken and in the subconscious, but we somehow know that there is something strong, that we believe in and which guides us. Understanding what your values are can be really helpful. When we are consciously aware of them, we are therefore more clear if they are violated by others. We may feel strong emotions against a person who breaks our rules, but they might not be their rules – we are all different.

Following her dream.

Having the confidence and self-belief to give up her career in catering, which came with a regular income, was tough but not as tough as Sarah thought it would be. The excitement of pursuing her passion, doing something creative, that she had always found herself drifting back to throughout her life, gave her an inner reassurance that what she was doing was the right thing for her.

If she ever did feel that doubt or self-questioning creeping in she reminded herself of what she had left behind, the hot sticky kitchens, a busy London location. These were great reminders of what she had moved from and how her future life was going to be so much more fulfilling. This is a great technique, reminding yourself what you left behind and what you are moving towards. Being able to visualise the future, and how that will be, helps keep you focused on the goal and where you are heading.

Being clear on where she was heading enabled Sarah to develop a plan to get there. Being a person who works on what the worst-case scenario might be, she then worked back from that to help mitigate against it. Income was a challenge so she initially offered her services to her previous employer in the catering business as a consultant working part time. She would be earning a similar amount of money, but without the extra hassle and stress; knowing that this was supporting her to follow her dream, made the work feel easier as it now had a higher purpose.

Alongside this, Sarah got a job as a picture framer, obtained a diploma in Arts Management, designed and sold printed T-shirts *and* made and sold papier-mâché art at Camden market. All this came from her previous experiences and talents.

Sarah's journey wasn't without the odd setback. Twice her husband got relocated, initially to Wiltshire and then to Devon – each time she had to adapt and find a different way to follow her passion. What she gained from this was the understanding that her work needed to be flexible and transferable; once she understood this, Sarah was able to develop her career around these requirements, ensuring that any future move would fit with the new model of working.

The relocation to Devon enabled her to refocus her career development again, taking a year out to enhance her creative knowledge and skills. Sarah combined an Art Foundation Course in Exeter with continuing to make and sell her creative work. This really worked with her passion of being creative, although at times she did feel a little lonely. After exhausting Radio 4 for company she decided to take up a teaching role in art and photography in a centre for young and disabled adults. Photography had never featured in Sarah's creative area before and it was only when she turned up for the position that they asked her if she could set up a darkroom. Whether it was naivety, or Sarah's zest for life that took over, but she replied that she could, thinking that it was just a question of turning off the light!

Being a person who has regularly found herself in challenging situations and often in an area that she didn't previously have any idea about, Sarah took the challenge on with mixed emotions, one of both excitement and terror. Using her entrepreneurial skills she found somebody who did know about darkrooms and got him to teach her, thinking that this was again another investment into her future creative career. Having mastered the photography, she worked with others in the centre to really support the attendees to be creative within their limitations – really stretching what was possible with the use of technology and a drive to help them create their own art. Many pieces of this art were displayed on the walls in beautiful frames created by Sarah – another skill being put to use.

Life often provides us with opportunities and experiences that we don't fully understand or appreciate until later. Sarah and her husband decided to start a family, she became pregnant, all was going well and she continued to work with her creative skills. Then at four months she suddenly found she was unable to stand. At this stage her art work was based on heavy materials, concrete, glass and lights, so she could no longer physically continue as she was so restricted in her movement. But of course, fortunately, the centre was accessible by wheel chair. Initially when Sarah couldn't walk she had no idea what was happening to her and irrational thoughts flooded into her head; she thought she had some terrible illness and that she would never see her unborn child. She was terrified of not being able to do something that had been so natural, something that she had taken for granted, being able to walk again.

Working at the disabled centre helped her physically, although it was the emotional side that she found most challenging. Having a supportive husband and mother definitely helped and another technique was to have a huge outpour, a big cry, once a week which then helped her keep stable for the week ahead. She took it one week at a time, recognising when she needed support, which being the independent person she was, was a challenge.

Sam, her first son, arrived and 21 months later was followed by Josh. During the second pregnancy her hips gave way again, meaning she had to cope with being in the wheel chair, being pregnant and having a small baby, so even more of a challenge.

Sarah now knew she needed another vision for what her life would look like in the future. She had no idea what it would look like but had faith that it would evolve, if she consciously wanted it to, and she started searching for the vision, as she had in the past.

Knowing that waiting around wasn't how her life had evolved to date, Sarah developed a new idea, Letters to Santa, where your child writes to Santa and they receive a personalised letter in the post, something she could do whilst her mobility was limited and whilst she was being a mum to her sons. Her creative desire and limited mobility led her to get the paints out with the boys at home. They tended to get stuck straight into an activity before Sarah had really set it all up and then, being boys, preferred to run down the hallway still covered in paint creating new patterns on the walls – so much more fun than sitting at the table with paints and paper.

To get herself and the boys out of the house Sarah tried all sorts of classes – music, gym, playgroups and crèches. But there was never a creative club to go to. So, eureka moment, the vision appeared, to set up and develop creative classes. This was where her career would go next, something flexible to fit round the boys and still playing to her creative passion. The vision had appeared so she set to work on the plan.

While moving house and just four months after having her second son she was up and running with her creative classes for children – the venue her kitchen table – a cottage industry in the making. Her drive and passion pushed back others' comments and resistance. People often commented that she was mad, not long being a mum for the second time, just beginning to walk again, her mobility nowhere near what it had been. But to Sarah it felt like the right thing to do, to combine her passion and talent with her new role as a mum.

When you get an idea you need to consider who to share it with, as often others will try to deter you or put you off. This is quite different from somebody who might support you with constructive comments to consider and make it work. They will often make encouraging comments about your ability to do this new project. Sarah had the ability to shield herself from negative comments because she believed in herself. Having been successful previously in developing a creative career for herself and dealing with set-backs, she knew that she would be able to do it again despite her physical limitations and having two boys to bring up.

Throughout her pregnancies Sarah was very up and down emotionally due to not having her mobility. She was a person who was full of energy and had actively taken part in physical activities, running, cycling, swimming – even walking the Three Peaks. I can't imagine what that would be like – to be so restricted and confined. Personally I was a nightmare to live with when I had a small operation that impacted on my mobility – Sarah didn't know if she would ever walk again. She felt tethered and frustrated with no release for all her energy.

Becoming a mum is difficult enough but for her to lose the use of her legs at the same time must have been horrendous.

She escaped with her boys to various clubs for company and to find conversation and mental stimulus, rather than being confined to the house which would have been easier for her physically. She knew, too, her boys needed the interaction and experiences as well as her, so she struggled to get herself out and about with the hope that she would enjoy the adult interaction. She often came away feeling worse as people for some reason didn't respond to Sarah making conversation, making her feel even more isolated and frustrated and sad.

Not letting this set her back, she used the time to observe and understand how the children interacted, what they responded to and didn't, what the parents seemed to enjoy and what motivated them. She thought about how the classes were run and what worked and what didn't and why – feeding her broader understanding and underlying vision. This gave her a purpose and reason for attending, so when the conversation didn't seem to flow she had a different reason to go for herself not just for the benefit of the boys.

Sarah ended up having three children, at one stage all were under three with the youngest two waking regularly through the night. Sleep is often the thing that enables us to rebalance, get things back into perspective, makes us feel a little more hopeful now we have more energy. Sarah didn't get this. She was also restricted in her physical ability and her passion for being creative wasn't truly being fulfilled. It was emerging slowly through the new club she had created, but she still felt there was something missing, that there was more she could do; this occasionally niggled in the background when she got time to reflect and think about the future.

Having that dream to hold onto while she was restricted and tired and irritable gave her hope and allowed her the opportunity to focus on something more, something better in the future. No doubt that old song *Wonderful Life* came back into her head a few times, and the words about life being what you make it.

Sarah's husband got relocated again, this time to Loughborough. She said 'that's OK', the key was always understanding that the career plan needed to be flexible and able to move. With that in mind she was positive that she would be able to set it up again in a new location based at home. The house sale fell through on the day they were due to exchange contracts. Having nowhere to live with three boys in a new location was a big set back, so getting accommodation quickly was the immediate priority. They ended up in student accommodation on a busy road which was not an ideal setting for a home or a business venture.

Sarah found the move more emotionally challenging than she probably realised she would – yet another change of address after things were just beginning to go in the right direction for her. She was also emotionally drained from all the physical challenges and then fighting to ensure she regained the ability to walk again. Doing all this whilst bringing up three boys and with little sleep, clearly drew on Sarah's reserves. Missing the home, with the nearness of the sea, which she had built for herself and the family, this seemed to be the final thing that she didn't feel able to battle any more. The first year in Loughborough was a real challenge and Sarah was quite ill; just running out of energy to pursue her dreams for a while.

What this time did give her was the time to think about the whole of her life and what she wanted in totality. Adding to the creative dream of her business, and being able to combine her passion around her children, was to be able to live where she wanted to live. She realised that the environment and being by the sea was as important to her as her career.

She set herself a goal of setting up ten franchises and being able to live in Devon again. Being able to see what success looked like for the whole of her needs enabled her to refocus and find her energy again.

So Sarah dusted off the model she had developed in Devon and started again with vigour in her living room. Sarah, being passionate about what she did, was infectious and soon found she was in demand and she outgrew the living room and took the next step and rented space in the leisure centre, the library and the science museum. Taking that leap from her living room was both exciting and terrifying; this was moving into serious business stuff as opposed to a hobby where mums came round to enjoy it too in her home. Yes, she was getting paid for it but she had not really ventured into anything so big before. All those hours of observation in the children's clubs had paid off, and Sarah combined her understanding of the children and parents with her talents to create a winning business model.

Sarah developed into doing parties and found she was in demand more than she could personally cope with. Thinking beyond just her and how she might be able to expand the business, was what often filled her head when she found any spare time. When her eldest son started school she found herself with her first creative franchise awarded.

Five years later her husband got head hunted again to return to Devon. Sarah no doubt cheered as she could see the opportunity to achieve another aspect of her dream, find the ideal house to make a home and be near the sea again.

On the business front she left Leicestershire with six franchises and she sold hers. The weekend before she left she was given the award of Businesswoman of the Year in Leicestershire. She was recognised for what she had achieved as a businesswoman, despite the setbacks and personal difficulties. A different story to the one when she had arrived.

Not long after, Sarah woke up in Devon in her new home and realised that she had her goal of ten franchises, and was living in Devon by the sea – exactly what she had set out to achieve. Sarah describes how goals have helped her achieve throughout her life – how being attuned to what you are looking for enables you to find it so much more easily. It's a bit like saying think of a red car: you find them so much more easily when you are focused on what you are looking for. Sarah is so right – our subconscious, if given direction through goal setting and being clear on what you want, can help steer you.

Sarah's focus shifted on her return to Devon. She took a big step and actually stopped running her own franchise, no longer doing the actual creative element. She realised now what had been so powerful in her role whilst in Africa when she ran the co-operative for the women. It was about supporting and providing the opportunity for other women who wanted to balance their work life with their children and do something that they enjoyed.

Making 'Creative Station' a household name for creative activities and inspiring young imaginations, was Sarah's new mission. She recruited a 'Dream Catcher' to help with the franchise enquiries which were received as demand was growing.

With this new focus and vision she still managed to balance her home life and make the boys central to how she worked.

Then she was faced with a whole new set of challenges – two of her key suppliers went bust within a three week period. Being somebody who always looked at worst-case scenarios and planned for them, she had a back-up supplier for all her main supplies. Keeping reliable and high quality products for her franchisees was vital to keep up her reputation and success. But she also realised at this stage with 23 franchises and the interest continuing through the country, she may have to make a difficult choice.

Running the business from home, even with other members of staff, was one that she felt enabled her to really support the boys and allow her to balance motherhood with being a business woman quite nicely. This had been the model all the way through – work from home to fit it round the boys' requirements.

Crunch time! Sarah needed to take on more staff to deal with the ever-increasing business. No longer could it all fit in the home office and this meant moving out. Not only was this against what she thought was right, but the finance to support this extra cost was a real challenge. This put the costs up seven times higher than they had been previously. She needed help with cash flow. Two banks turned her down, which might have been enough for some people to say 'Well what's the point?' and give up. This is not the case with Sarah, this was her passion, her vision for the future and she carried on until she found a bank to buy into her vision and support her.

The biggest challenge for Sarah at this time was connected to her value of role modelling what she was selling – a successful working mum who has a business based at home. She was no longer going to be able to live this message and it was a mental challenge that might have limited her further expansion and prevented her from delivering that inspirational dream to support other mums to do just that.

Interestingly when she was going through this mental challenge her body gave her another one. She obtained a running injury; having fully regained her mobility, she was back to being active again. However this injury meant she was unable to stand for more than five minutes and walk for more than ten metres. Sarah reflects on the fact that an element of familiarity to her is that when she needs to make a difficult decision, and doesn't seem to be able to make it or is having difficulty getting to it, her body gives her the opportunity to do so by giving her a *physical* challenge. This creates the time and space for her to really deal with the decision. Often our bodies give us a signal, a message, nudging us to take time out for important aspects of our lives that need attention. The knack is recognising them and, like Sarah, to take the time to consider them and then move positively forward.

I have a question which I often ask my clients when they are hit by a difficulty which reminds me of Sarah's positive insight to this situation. 'What is the positive from this situation?' Although it may be difficult to see, if you search within yourself you will usually find something that helps you grow and change. Or in Sarah's case, stop and take some time out, to give this important decision some considered time to explore how she was truly feeling about it. Which then enabled her to find a solution that would work for her.

Which she did – she found an old farm building seven minutes from home where she could see the sea from her office window, which is an inspiration for her. The property had the extra storage facility which was becoming a big challenge and allowed her to recruit another member of staff.

Being a goal-setter, she then challenged herself to double the business to sort out the cash flow aspect. She achieved this sooner than she thought with 46 franchises and a good cash flow which will support taking the business to the next level.

And Sarah seems well on the way to achieving the next level – looking at new and inspiring ways to attract new mums; four 'Inspiring Imaginations' conferences; the 'Creation Station' branded goods; and a shop to be launched soon.

Sarah still struggles with her hip; she has to limit her high heels to a sensible level and is still unable to run. But unless she is away, she manages to be home for 3pm when the boys arrive home and achieves the dream that she painted for herself.

Key areas of resilience demonstrated

Self-efficacy

Despite times being difficult, unfamiliar or fearful, Sarah had an inner belief in her ability to deal with the situation. This strength of knowing pulled her through. There were times when it wavered but when she reconnected to her abilities and what she had previously achieved this rebuilt her confidence in herself and moved her forward.

Purpose and clarity of direction

There were times in Sarah's story where this was vague and unclear. However, she listened to her instincts and allowed her intuition to guide her. We aren't always crystal clear about our future direction but we may have a sense that something will help us move closer to it. There were times when Sarah allowed herself to dream and play with what the future might hold, visualising all aspects of her life and allowing herself to play with that fantasy. A move back to Devon, a house by the sea, a business where she could combine her creative talents and help other mums to do the same. Having a longer term view of her future enabled her to make good short term goals that strengthened the likelihood of achieving the bigger goal. Sarah didn't rest when she achieved it, she set herself some further stretching goals to keep positively moving and expanding her future dream.

Problem solving, adaptability and growth mindset

Sarah demonstrated her ability to solve barriers that she came across. As a child she adapted her plans to obtain sweets. She found ways to raise money to achieve her dream of going on Operation Raleigh. As an adult, growing her business, she found new ways to develop and grow it.

In the early days she became curious about what satisfied the parents and created enjoyment at the various clubs she attended. Being curious enabled her to observe and be open-minded, expanding her understanding and knowledge which all became useful later.

Support

Being an independent woman who had a view that taking personal responsibility was the key to making things happen, challenged her ability to accept and ask for help. Losing the use of her legs created a situation where she did have to ask for support. This has helped her to understand the balance around being very independent and making things happen and having key people who can assist you.

She also learnt what she needed and allowed herself to have it: the big cry once a week. The time when life became too much she listened to what she needed and went with it, without losing sight of her dreams.

Reminders for me through writing this chapter

Sarah is a great example of tapping into your strengths, understanding what they are, listening to them. She constantly gravitated back towards being able to use her artistic talents. Reminds me to constantly think about how I use my strengths and what can I do to enhance them further.

The other great thing I take from Sarah's story is her relentlessness around dreaming and setting goals and making sure she constantly moves towards them. A great reminder in connection with me getting this book finished. What's my next goal?

Strategies to develop resilience Sarah-style

Self-efficacy

Developing a strength, becoming really good at something, developing mastery of a talent. Sarah constantly kept coming back to her creative side, she discovered it as a child and then nurtured it through her life in different ways, successfully getting to a position where she combines her talents with a successful business. We don't all have to do that but knowing what our natural talents and strengths are will help us fit more into our lives and ultimately make us feel more at one, happier with ourselves and generally more productive.

What do we mean by a strength? It's when you feel totally absorbed in something, something you are good at, that you enjoy doing and you find it energises you. We may be good at something but it's not a strength if it doesn't energise you; in fact using it can drain you as it takes more energy to be good at it. The key is that you are both good and energised. When using it you will tend to feel more authentic, at one, as it feels right.

So how do you unlock a strength? Ask yourself the following:

- What do you enjoy doing?
- What do you find yourself doing when you lose track of time, become absorbed in?
- What did you find yourself naturally doing as a child?
- When you feel at one, what are you doing?
- If you had lots of spare time, what would you gravitate to doing?
- What can't you help yourself doing?

These suggestions may help you unlock them or you can take strengths assessments online.

Strengths assessments

Clifton Strengths Finder developed by Clifton and colleagues at Gallup.

www.strengthsfinder.com

VIA Inventory of Strengths developed by leading positive psychologists Christopher Peterson and Martin Seligman.

www.viastrengths.org

Realise2 developed through CAPP and Alex Linley, this not only identifies your strengths but your unrealised strengths.

www.realise2.org

When developing your resilience, knowing your strengths and developing them over time will enable you to become even better at them. Minimising the areas that drain your energy will ensure your energy levels have a better chance of being high. You will enjoy life through utilising your strengths more, you will feel more at one with yourself; more confidence will grow as you continue to develop these skills. When a difficulty comes your way go to your strengths and ask yourself which strengths would be helpful to use now.

Do it yourself, if it doesn't work initially then adapt and try something different. Your successful achievement will raise your self-efficacy. Take the responsibility as Sarah did that you have the ability to determine your life – yes, you may get setbacks and difficulties but ultimately you can move your life forward.

Visualise success. Give your brain a strong picture about what success looks like. Tap into the power of your subconscious mind, allow yourself to dream and build strong images around your future. Your brain works in images and colour, spend time on building those images, and strengthen them by drawing pictures or images, in colour. Brian Mayne has developed a fantastic technique, that taps into your subconscious brain, called Goal Mapping, www.liftinternational.com. Allow yourself time to dream, we best tap into our creative side when we aren't busy and our heads aren't full of stuff. Plan some downtime and see what emerges in your head.

Purpose and clarity of direction

Experience 'flow'. Flow is the mental state of operation in which a person performing an activity is fully immersed in a feeling of energised focus, full involvement, and enjoyment in the process of the activity. Proposed by Mihály Csikszentmihályi, the positive psychology concept of flow has been widely referenced across a variety of fields. When in flow you will feel enjoyment, you will be totally submerged in it, not see other things around you. Notice when you become totally immersed in something and have lost the track of time and feel energised after doing it. Recognise what it is and navigate your life to be able to do more of it. Sarah found she was in flow when she was being creative, constantly gravitating towards it. This combined with her relentless goal setting helped propel her forward and achieve.

Problem solving, adaptability and growth mindset

Develop your creativity. We tend to stick to similar paths and habits. Do something different and open up your mind to new experiences. This will help stimulate your creativity. Sarah often found herself doing new things that she hadn't done before, printing T-shirts, photography, all helping stimulate her in new and different directions.

Develop your curiosity. Learn to ask great questions; successful people ask great questions to find out more and open up their thinking and knowledge so they have more information to be able to make decisions. Another way of being curious is to take time to observe others as Sarah did when she was watching the children at the different play groups, helping her to understand what was important to them.

Support

For Sarah learning how to accept what she needed only came when she had a physical crisis. This is a fairly dramatic way to get used to accepting support. Although it's great to be truly responsible for yourself, it doesn't mean you can't ask for assistance from others. Learn when help from others would be beneficial, take time to consider your current situation and goals and ask yourself where would support or help be useful and who might you ask for it? Explore the reason for not asking for help; what are you assuming that's getting in the way of you asking? Is that assumption true? Really? If you knew that you would receive unsolicited assistance, what would you do?

Faith is not one thing or two or three things. It is an indivisible totality of beliefs that inspire me. – Helen Keller.

Chapter 7

JULIE'S STORY – REALISING IT WASN'T MY FAULT

The time has come to start my story. It has been floating around in my head for a few days now, but for some reason I hadn't wanted to make a start. This morning, having just been to the gym, I had a conversation with a 69-year-old gentleman, whom I often chat with, and he told me about the book that he's writing. It sounds like a great story about his rather chequered but interesting life. This then inspired me to get pen to paper as they say. It is funny how the universe often sends you little messages or things to help. I think this was definitely one of those so it would be right to take notice and get on with my story.

We start in Bury St Edmunds; I was working as a HR Manager with Marks and Spencer, with a fantastic store management team and a manager who knew how to have fun to balance the hard work we did. Despite having a great job and great people to work with, something was missing. I had my own house so I was away from my childhood home but I had been since I was 18 following my career with Marks and Spencer. I had developed new friendships both at home and in Bury St Edmunds. However I felt lonely. I'm not sure I truly understood this at the time. I just felt at times sad and that despite my energy to arrange social things and have a full life, there was something missing.

I was at an age where friends were getting married and children were coming along. And although I knew I didn't want children yet, I had too much to achieve with the career, there seemed to be a gap in my life.

I met Steve who was an aircraft engineer in the RAF and we had fun, enjoyed ourselves and developed a relationship. I fell in love. Steve was not the type of man you would have put me with – for starters he was ginger and I had never found ginger men attractive, but it's all down to personal choice. We lived together in my house until I moved to Burton-on-Trent with work and he moved to Lossiemouth to be stationed up there. We only saw each other every three or four weeks which was exceptionally hard, but I did get to see Scotland – the Northern Lights, the whisky, amazing scenery in the summer, but my God not great in the winter when it's dark for most of the day; you can only stay in bed for so long, even if you are young and in love.

Finally came the day of the wedding which was magical – just as a wedding should be – and I walked to the village church with my dad, with the full array of bridesmaids, flowers, the works. I was so emotional – finally getting to the point when I could be with Steve I couldn't get my vows out without tears. At last we were going to start our life together again after the distances and difficulties.

Steve was coming out of the Forces and we lived together initially in Burton-on-Trent before we moved to Leicester, as I again moved roles within Marks and Spencer.

I imagined life together would be magical. All that waiting and dreaming had left me with a wonderful picture in my mind. However it didn't quite turn out like that. Steve found it exceptionally difficult to deal with life outside the RAF routine, not finding employment until my dad gave him a sales job for his company. However this didn't work out either. Steve had extreme difficulty adapting to Civvy Street, as they say in the Forces. Not having everything planned and decided for him began to take its toll; he struggled with the job, made mistakes, found it almost too much for him to handle. While he was struggling with this, I fell pregnant. It was planned but I think this new responsibility on top of him struggling to adjust to life outside the RAF became too much. Steve started drinking in secret. I didn't actually know at this stage, I just knew he was ill but resisting support from me and I didn't know why.

In hindsight I suppose I should have seen the signs: when we initially lived together, we did drink lots but often in your youth, with not too many commitments, you do party hard. I remember now a sign that I definitely missed. I came home from work one day and found the hat stand smashed at the bottom of the stairs and Steve sleeping off the drink. He had fallen down the stairs and not even felt it, he didn't even realise what he had done until he woke hours later and found a large gash across his side from the broken wood. At the time I just put it down to the life in the RAF being one of play hard.

I had obviously blocked this from my mind until years later when I started to unpick the clues; I was surprised and so were others that being a bright intelligent woman I had not seen it coming.

Steve was an alcoholic but this wasn't truly realised until much later. It is worth sharing with you the kind of things I experienced and how I felt whilst living with an alcoholic.

Living with Steve for the majority of the time was fun and enjoyable, he was rather childlike in his fun and often made me laugh; he was loving and affectionate and delighted at the thought of becoming a parent. Although I knew I was the one with the responsibilities of the house and the consistent income, for most of the time it didn't matter, we enjoyed life and were excited as most parents are about our unborn child. There were odd situations during the pregnancy that started to upset me; I'd talk to Steve, things would be all right for a while, then the next situation would occur. He'd apologise and promise to make things better. At this stage he was still working for my dad but I was concerned about his progress with the job as I knew he was finding it difficult and fitting into the normal world of work and taking responsibility for himself and his actions was not something he found easy. I also knew that dad was not one to give out charity and if you worked for him you had to cut the mustard but he was prepared to give people a chance. I found myself constantly balancing the requirements of these two aspects, supporting Steve, but trying to push him to deliver in the role as I knew it would be difficult for dad to have to justify keeping a poor performing relative on the team.

I remember being heavily pregnant and still working and I'm not sure what situation had occurred but I felt the need to drive home to my parents for support, so got in the car on a Sunday and drove two hours to get to somewhere safe. I was daunted enough about becoming a parent and really didn't know how to deal with the situation I was in where my husband and soon to be father of my child was at times drinking excessively. He seemed not to be accepting the responsibilities he had, happily passing them all to me.

I arrived at my parents and told them that I was struggling and didn't know what to do and that I found Steve difficult to deal with; at this stage I didn't share my concerns about his drinking; I wasn't really sure myself that I had accepted or understood them. This must have made it difficult for my parents to understand what was going on and why I felt like I did. I was sent firmly back by my dad and told that it takes two to make a marriage work and that I had better start discussing these issues with Steve. I spent the whole journey back home crying, even now as I write this I am feeling tearful. I didn't want to go back. I wanted to be pampered and looked after – I was pregnant *and* probably in my subconscious knew at this stage that this relationship was in a bad way and not one in which to bring a child. Also not sharing the reality of this situation with others prevented people really being able to offer help and left me feeling alone and carrying a huge burden.

As the journey continued, the tears stopped and in my normal common sense way, I gave myself a talking to. I was the one going to have to fix this problem. I had a responsibility to my unborn child that I needed to get things right so he/she was born into a better place than it was at the moment.

I returned home and Steve was oblivious to the fact that I'd been missing and that there was anything wrong. Being exhausted emotionally I decided two could play the same game and got myself something to eat and went to bed. Head in the sand – I know – but it felt good just to hope it would all 'be better in the morning'.

We were back into the pretend world again. The next specific incident I remember was the birth of my wonderful daughter. Steve was with me for the 23 hours of labour, being supportive and loving. The baby arrived, I didn't know at this stage what sex it was but my first words were 'is it ginger!'. Like I said, I always had an issue with ginger; auburn lovely, but ginger doesn't really do it for me. I should have stuck to that rule and I probably wouldn't have been in this situation. And just for the record it was a girl, no she's not ginger, but blonde with lovely brown eyes – takes after mum.

The next day while I'm bewildered about being a parent, Steve doesn't appear. He finally turns up all smiles as though nothing is out of the ordinary in the evening. I asked where he'd been. He just replied he went to wet the baby's head. As was his pattern, he brought lavish gifts. I didn't realise then but the pattern emerged – went out drinking, returns with some expensive gift thinking all will be OK. This time it was a gold necklace. I knew he would have been alone when he was out drinking, as all his friends and relatives lived away from Leicester. Emily, my daughter, needed all my attention so that's where I spent my efforts and again chose to ignore what I feared. Anyway life was too full and exciting with my new bundle of joy, and as a new parent I didn't have a clue what to do so had to learn how to trust my instincts as well as listen to lots of advice and pick out the bits that felt right for me and Emily.

As I was the major income earner of the two of us I had to go back to work after four months; to be fair I always knew I would be a working mum, although the ideal might not have been full time in a management career with new challenges. We recruited a nanny, well I say *we* but I mean me. Michelle was a godsend, she was flexible to be there when I wasn't. For the majority of the time it was down to her and me to care for Emily. Steve got involved but I suppose I knew that I didn't want to rely on him as I never knew when he would let me down so I worked around it.

Although Steve was loving and caring as a father with Emily, the responsibility aspect of becoming a parent and having to take care of somebody who couldn't care for herself just sent him spiralling down. He had difficulty taking responsibility for himself: I did the house, parenting and the relationship. I did this to ease the burden and enable him to concentrate on himself and his job. I was trying to protect him from as much of the reality as possible, which was probably not the best thing to do, but it enabled me to be in control for as much as possible and deal with being a working mother of a young child. I was managing all the financial aspects, the household and the child care. I felt better if I could anticipate the potential issues and head them off. When I didn't, Steve hit the vodka bottle. At this time I often felt helpless and cried a lot. But I would think back to the day when I travelled home from my parents when I was pregnant. I knew it was down to me somehow to sort out this mess.

Eventually, after a particular incident, I had to fully confront Steve with a different approach. Steve went missing. He had popped out on a Sunday I think to get something from the DIY shop but five hours later he still hadn't returned and I was distraught with worry. I went to a friend of mine and left Emily while I went looking, aimlessly driving the streets of Leicester, to try and find him. I did, slumped over the wheel of his car. I was unable to raise him and at this stage, probably due to the fact that we had never really addressed his drinking and I was in denial, was concerned that he was seriously ill. I rang for the ambulance. They came along with the police. Steve was taken to A&E and I followed after the police had checked his car and found nothing. Steve had the full ECG tests, etc, and they found nothing wrong so I took him home and got him to bed, then went via Steve's car to pick up Emily. Why did I go via the car – because I knew that the police had missed something. There was really nothing wrong with Steve other than the fact that he had a drink problem and I had to find the evidence – to make it a reality. Living with an alcoholic for some reason makes you search for the truth about the drinking and you need to find the evidence. After this day there were many times I went routing round the garage in the most bizarre of places to find the vodka bottle. You become almost obsessed with finding evidence – I'm not sure why, as when I did, it made me feel rock bottom; again he'd let himself and me down.

Anyway, yes, I found the vodka bottle. In a way it was a shame the police never found it. I collected Emily, made up some story about Steve not being well to my friends and returned home to get Emily fed and in bed before I sat down again and cried – not knowing what to do, feeling again helpless, but realising that this time I had to get Steve to realise the seriousness of his situation and that I would support him to seek help and recover from this.

Why did I make up the story to my friends? I found myself doing this a lot as things progressed. I felt the shame, I felt that Steve being an alcoholic was my fault. Irrational I know now, but I did feel I had failed at my marriage. I felt it was because of me he was an alcoholic. Later on when my friends said to me we never knew, why didn't you let us know or ask for help, I had worked through this and I explained to them how for some reason I had taken on the responsibility of the problem and the fact that I needed to sort it. It was only later that I realised that I couldn't do that and that Steve needed to sort it out. This in hindsight has been a fantastic lesson in really getting me to understand where to spend your energy around wanting to change things. You can only change you, not others; you can adapt your response and reaction to others but you don't control them so you can't change them. So spend your energy on what you can influence and change. From a support aspect, you can offer advice and discuss things, but if the person you are trying to help doesn't see it or want it you can't get them to take it. Frustrating absolutely but I learnt my lesson back then and now offer support in a different way.

After this event Steve registered with Alcoholics Anonymous. We – yes we, as I went along – spoke to his doctor. For me this was a route to help Steve and I felt there was a way forward that would bring Steve back.

Every Tuesday, off he went to AA and it was not for a while, me being the trusting individual I am and believing Steve when he told me he wanted to sort himself out, that I discovered he wasn't going to AA – but the pub. But he was careful not to drink too much. Steve lived in a different world at times – one that was quite imaginary, where life was wonderful and which just fed his denial about the issue.

His drinking got worse and I got more concerned, so much so that I would try to do anything but leave Emily with him, especially when

I worked on a Saturday. Working in retail I had to work alternate Saturdays. There was one particular weekend coming up when I had no local support and I still had not told anybody about Steve's problem. But Emily came first so I thought I would invite his mother down and then at the same time let her know what was happening with Steve to see if she could talk to him and get him to face the truth.

She came, so Emily was safe. However, though I asked for support, on this difficult and delicate matter, I didn't get it: Steve's mother didn't want to upset the apple cart and talk to him about it and, if I'm honest with myself, she was probably going through the stage I had been through – head in the sand, this can't be true. At the time I felt let down and angry; I had finally got around to asking for some help and it felt like I had been pushed back into 'Well it's down to you, Julie', so I shut that route for support off and went back to coping alone.

Steve and I did what most people do in a relationship that isn't all that you'd like it to be – we carried on, went on holiday thinking the sunshine would make it all better. But the real issue was not being dealt with.

Around this time I remember supporting the hairdresser from work – yes, this was the good old days when Marks and Spencer had a hairdresser. The business had decided that this role could no longer continue and it would mean either a relocation into a different role or a redundancy package. The hairdresser, Anne, was really well presented and attractive, young for her age, and somebody who always had a positive outlook on life, well on the outside. While helping her through this particular time she shared with me what her life was like outside of work. She was married to an alcoholic, had been for 20 years, and felt she had never really found true happiness. Through our discussions she decided that this was the catalyst to help her find a new happier life; she had got choices and could move on from her husband. Initially the situation was daunting, as she was either going to have to work in a job she didn't like away from hairdressing, or not have a job, but out of this came empowerment to make a choice that freed her from the current situation where she had felt there were no other options.

She left Marks and Spencer, taking the redundancy package, and she left her husband. When I saw her months later she looked even more amazing, a definite inner glow about her; she was in love, she had a new younger man and was enjoying her freedom and happiness.

Anne's story is significant in that when the time was right I remembered her plight and how she had spent 20 years trying to support and help her husband, all to no avail as he wasn't ready to deal with his illness. I do think things are sent to you to help you and helping Anne with her choices later helped me with mine. Odd that I was able to support and help her make the choices that created her future happiness yet at the time I wasn't able to help myself in the best way.

Like Anne, I had a significant event that finally made me change where we were.

I had no option one Saturday afternoon but to leave Steve in charge of Emily, full of dread and anxiety all day and ringing just about every hour to check he was OK. I managed to get my work done and return home.

I arrived to find him bathing Emily while drunk. By now she was 13 months old but even so he had no idea whether she was safe or not, his reactions were delayed and he could hardly stand let alone be able to save her if she had slipped beneath the water. Thinking about it now makes my stomach churn and I feel sick just remembering what I found, and about what might have happened. All my motherly instincts kicked in and I rescued Emily from the situation. Luckily she was fine and she hadn't come to any harm but for me this was the crystallising event. I knew I would never be able to forgive him for putting her life in danger, children are innocent and deserve to be protected by their parents. He had created a dangerous situation and not considered anybody but himself in the fact that he got drunk before he had taken her for a bath.

Later on I realised that I had been able to put up with all sorts along the journey of trying to support Steve and help him to realise where he was and what he needed to do to get better. But I couldn't deal with the fact that he had treated his own child in this way. So remembering Anne and her choices, I also made a choice that meant separating from Steve. I could no longer risk him being part of Emily's and my life.

Steve moved out.

Within weeks he ended up getting stopped for drinking and driving; he was so much over the limit that he was immediately locked up in Leicester prison. Being the only person locally to support him I took along the toiletry essentials; I never thought I'd be visiting my husband, who I had decided to leave, in prison. But I had loved him and felt the need to support him in this difficult time.

This also brought relief for me. While he was in prison he was out of the way and I could concentrate on Emily and work – notice I didn't say me, which is actually where I probably needed to spend some time. However, being a single working parent at this time and being away from close friends and family, I just went through the motions of getting through work. Emily filled my time, making me exhausted and so I slept, for the first time in a long time.

While with Steve I often lay awake for hours playing through in my mind what were we going to do, how could I get out of this mess we were in financially as well as his drinking issues? We were in a difficult situation due to Steve drinking the joint account money which paid for the bills and mortgage. If I wasn't worrying about aspects like this then I'd be lying awake waiting for the inevitable, Steve pissing the bed. Many times did I lay there knowing that due to the state he was in he would wet himself. I got really good at reading the signs and kicking him out of bed before it occurred, so he ended up lying in his own wee for the rest of the night. I'm not proud of myself for this but I was so angry that I felt he deserved it and I was hoping that waking up cold and covered in his own wee might shock him into doing something different. But it never did. He refused to move out of our bed and I was rather stubborn so put myself through this torture until, quite late on, I did move to the spare bed. My stubbornness often got in the way of sensible decisions. As a teenager I even missed out on seeing Julio Iglesias on the beach because I was being stubborn – but that's another story. I'm a lot more flexible now.

I started to believe that there was a better way and we, Emily and I, could make a go of this. I still felt I had failed in getting Steve better but knew my efforts needed to be focused on Emily.

Then Steve came out of jail and wanted to see Emily. After all the dread and fear had rushed through me I thought he is her father and maybe he has realised the seriousness of the situation he is in and the stint in jail will have helped him move forward. He came to see her and was lovely, as he could be; he also wanted to move back in but I explained that it was beyond that and I couldn't go back. He went for a walk to the shop to get something for me and came back two hours later collapsing in my lounge, totally out cold, slumped on the floor behind the sofa. He'd found the vodka bottle again.

I remember thinking that even though I had made difficult choices he was still here ruining my life; I couldn't take any more and collapsed sobbing. Then Emily who was now 14 months old walked towards me and gave me a big hug. She knew at this early age I was upset and just needed a cuddle.

This helped remind me of who was important and we went out and enjoyed ourselves, leaving Steve slumped on the floor. I did think that he would come round and leave but when I returned and I fed, bathed and put Emily to sleep, he was still out cold. The anger kicked in, I got the empty vodka bottle and smashed it over his head. The built-up anger was so strong that I completely lost it.

I quickly realised the logic of the situation and was mortified that I might have physically hurt him. Luckily I hadn't, he was so conked out with the drink that he was relaxed and the blow didn't impact. I realised though that I needed some help.

This came in the form of Relate. We had registered with them when we were still together desperate as I was to try anything to help us work through the situation. Due to the huge demand on their services I didn't get an appointment with a counsellor until I had decided Steve and I were no longer a partnership. However they were extremely helpful now and they allowed me support despite the fact I was single.

How did it help?

- It gave me personal time for me. I found I was spending all my energy on holding it together, working and still performing in my role as HR Manager and looking after Emily. I had no time or space to really think about the impact of my relationship with Steve. I was just being busy and filling my time with activities rather than reflecting on how I felt about it all, which was exhausting.

- It gave me somebody completely objective to talk to. No judgments or personal views, just someone whom could ask some useful questions to really help me think about different aspects.

- It gave me a safe space to let my emotions out. I could just be me, I didn't have to be strong or professional or put a brave face on. And yes, the emotions flowed but it was rather healing in a way.

- It gave me time to unravel the feeling that it was all my fault and that I had failed at my marriage.

- It enabled me to understand my role in the relationship and how I couldn't take responsibility from Steve to make him better.

- Overall I grew as a person, understanding aspects around my relationship with my parents through this period as well as my relationship with Steve.

- Most importantly it enabled me to let go of the negative emotions attached to the situation: the 'why me?', the anger with Steve for putting me in this position.

Slowly I grew stronger through this period and felt like the weight was lifting slowly off my weary shoulders. I was able to enjoy work a little more as the team knew some of what I had been through and I was no longer trying to hold it all together without letting anybody else know.

I spent time out at my parents just escaping and building up my reserves again and allowing myself to be looked after a little which was exactly what I needed. It felt like an awfully long time since anybody had looked after me.

Once I had started to pull myself together I realised that financially I was in a mess. My savings had been depleted through bailing Steve out over the years, when he got into debt with his credit cards. He had also emptied the joint account, which we used to pay the mortgage and the nanny. And the income I was earning wasn't enough on my own to pay for everything. Shit! Another knock-back that for a while I had not felt strong enough to face and now that I could I wasn't sure what to do. I didn't feel up to moving and that wasn't going to be soon enough anyway. Michelle, the nanny, was a godsend and had helped me through the difficult dark times and become a constant for Emily that I didn't want to change. She needed some consistent support in her life other than me. And family and friends were too far away to help with the childcare.

I had only one option left to me and that was to talk to my parents. Being brought up as an independent child and from a background of 'You make your own way in the world', I was filled with dread about how I was going to broach this subject. Again I felt this was a sign of failure – having to ask my parents for some financial support at the age of 32.

I managed it and my parents were fantastic – offering to support me with the nanny payments so I could continue as I was for a while longer.

Failure appears a lot through this part of my journey and it has been interesting to understand its impact on me. It stopped me asking for help and support and potentially making my life, and maybe Steve's, easier through this difficult period. Thank goodness I learnt this lesson then and I am now able to ask for help more easily. I do still slip back into feeling I have to do it all but am more aware of when it is beginning to feel like too much and able to stop, rethink what I need and then ask others to help me. Ultimately this enables me to be more effective in helping others.

I also found music helpful as I was starting to get stronger. Music has always been in my life and I identify certain tunes with certain times. For example, play me ELO and I will go back to my childhood, travelling with my mum and brother to visit my dad in hospital in Sheffield, after a serious back operation. It must have been the music we always played on that journey and it takes me right back there with all the anxiety of whether my dad would be OK.

I remember once playing Robbie Williams really loud whilst on a long journey for work. It was his first album after he had broken away from Take That. And I remember feeling invigorated and alive and full of hope about the future, probably how Robbie felt. Music can be what we, as coaches, call an anchor, as I have discussed, taking us back to a previous memory and emotional connection. It can also be a real mood lifter if we use it effectively.

I started to let my friends in during this time and I remember escaping over the New Year period to a close friend – Sarah and her family. Again it was easy to just be me there and the fact that there were others to support with Emily also helped. They had a son, Joe, who had always wanted a younger sister. He soon discovered after having Emily, who at this stage was 15 months old and messed with his tidy bedroom and put his toys all over the place, that having a younger sister didn't seem so appealing. My friend was delighted by this as she didn't want any more children so we had done her a favour by getting Joe to change his mind. I let friends in to the real me; I had learnt how to and had gone through the journey with the counsellor and that enabled me to look at things differently. Getting rid of the shame and guilt enabled me to see things differently – not sure why I thought I would be judged harshly by my friends, but at times like this you don't always see things logically.

Julie rediscovers herself as a woman.

It was pre-Christmas time and I was still very raw and wouldn't have noticed if a gorgeous male model came into the room naked. My attraction antennae were well and truly switched off. In December, I and the Deputy Manager interviewed a man for a supervisor vacancy. He was somebody who had potential and a lovely nature about him – he would be a good balance to the generally strong female team that we had. Stephanie, the Deputy Manager, also assured me he was rather good looking and that it might be a pleasant experience to have an attractive man on the team. Did I notice? Like I said, if an amazing male model had walked in naked I wouldn't have batted an eye, as I was not in a place to appreciate the attractions of the opposite sex.

Stephanie had also split from her husband; by her thirties she had been with her husband from a young age and she took the approach that it was time to 'party' – she hadn't ever done that phase. Occasionally she would come round with a take-away pizza and a bottle of wine and we would laugh at her escapades as she explored the night scene of Leicester and the men in it.

Emily, thank goodness, kept me grounded on what was important and gave me a great excuse not to accompany Stephanie on her wild phase. They were great stories to listen to but not ones I felt I wanted to be part of.

Redeveloping yourself as a woman after being rejected by a husband is also another discovery phase. Although Steve hadn't left me for another woman, he had chosen drink as his companion. So rediscovering who I was as a single person and not just a mother and wife was a whole other part of my journey.

Well physically I looked fairly good; I had always been curvy and voluptuous but at that time had shed a few pounds with all the stress and worry. I started to feel good about how I looked. I started to think about meeting somebody else, when occupationally I had time to day dream what might be. Despite the difficulties I had been through, I knew I would meet someone and I had definitely not been put off the whole relationship experience. Some of this had come through the counselling sessions where I had been able to let go and move forward.

Well, I suddenly noticed Mark, the new supervisor that Stephanie had said was rather attractive. How had I not noticed before? He looked great in a suit, but even better when he took his jacket off. And I found myself walking on the sales floor more often to see him and wander over for a chat. We used to have management meetings and if he happened to sit next to me I felt the electricity between us. I was surprised that no one else noticed this.

At this time in Marks and Spencer it wasn't really the done thing for a senior member of management – me – to date a middle member of management – Mark, especially if you were in the same store. What was I to do?

I remember having a great chat one day with a fellow HR Manager about my dilemma and discussing what I could do next. The plan was to test the water as I had no idea what his views were. And although I knew he was also going through a divorce I had no idea whether there was anyone else for him.

The plan: to find an excuse to play the pathetic female and ask for his support on something. Well this was a bigger challenge than anybody can imagine. I had never played the pathetic female. What did you do? How were you meant to be? What could I be pathetic about? I had left home at 18 and fended pretty much for myself all along the way; my marriage to Steve was one where I had taken control and managed everything. Well the plan came together quite by chance; my car needed some attention and I thought great, stereotypical situation here, men always think females can't do the car thing and are taken advantage of at the garage. So I wander onto the sales floor, find Mark and strike up a conversation, telling him the story of how my car isn't working properly and I have no idea what it is and being a female on my own I'm a little concerned about where to take it and whether the garage would take advantage of me. This was all going amazingly well until a female colleague of Mark's and who I had not spotted, shouts up, 'What, take advantage of you, Julie, you've got to be kidding.' Had I been rumbled? What was I to do? I am unsure how I got out of this situation but Mark being the gentleman that he was took the car and brought me the keys back to my office later. I hadn't thought the next bit through; had he done it because he quite liked me or had he done it because he felt that his HR Manager had asked him and it was only polite to do so? How would I find out? What was I meant to do next? We'd not talked about this part when my friend and I had been hatching the plan. Just goes to show when planning you really need to cover all the angles and get the whole plan sketched out.

Again this part was a blur but I do remember I had bought him a chocolate animal from Thornton's as a thank-you. But I was still none the wiser.

The pressure of constantly making myself look stunning for work and holding myself back from the desire to touch Mark was immense. I knew I had to do something. Another plan. What this time? How could I be a little more direct without scaring him off or embarrassing myself if I had this all wrong? At the end of the day I was still his HR Manager and would have to work with him afterwards whatever happened. What surprises me looking back at this, is how I ever managed to summon up the courage to take the action I did. But as my fellow planner said, he was never going to approach me – he had more to lose with the position issue in Marks and Spencer – so it was up to me. Well that was a phrase actually I was quite comfortable with. As you know, that phrase had kicked me into action before on a route to finding something better than where I was.

I asked myself what was the worst-case scenario: he rejects me and I have to continue to work with him. From what I had learnt about him I felt he was a nice guy and wouldn't make this more difficult than it needed to be if that were the case.

What was the best-case scenario: well he too could feel like I do and want to explore it further.

What was the most realistic case? I wasn't too sure on this but the worst case, once I'd scaled it into something that was a little more realistic, didn't feel too bad either.

So what did I do? I decided to find a common subject to place him in the expert position again. We were both going through a divorce – all that legal stuff, very complicated – maybe this was a starter.

I went for a stroll on the sales floor, this time surveying the place well to ensure no hiding colleagues that were going to jeopardise my subtle, well not so subtle, plan in making the first move.

Great he's alone and nobody around. I make my approach all relaxed and by just starting up a general conversation, leading it on to his divorce and where he was with it all, then commenting on how I found it so confusing and would really appreciate his take on it all. Maybe we could have a coffee or lunch one day when we had a little more time to discuss it further.

He positively took the bait and we arranged to meet for lunch the following day in a nearby wine bar.

I didn't sleep much that night wondering where lunch was going to take us and did he really think I wanted to talk about the divorce. I had, whilst talking to the solicitor, had a shock about the whole custody issue. I didn't 'not want' Steve to see Emily. I never wanted Emily, in years to come, to say to me 'You never let me see my dad', but I did want to ensure her safety, so wanted to be able to put restrictions on how he could see her. Due to his alcoholism I only wanted him to see Emily with another responsible adult present – sensible you would think bearing in mind his record. I mean it wasn't just me saying he had a drink problem, he had been locked up in prison for the amount he had drunk whilst driving. So you would think that the legal system might help protect a child on this issue. No.

I could express my feelings in the papers that were being drawn up, but because Steve hadn't actually caused harm to Emily previously, I couldn't insist upon access restrictions.

However, I didn't really think this was a great subject to talk about with Mark, so what was I going to say and would the conversation naturally move on or was this meeting still a bit too work-like?

I remember not being able to concentrate all morning at work and I didn't dare go for a walk on the floor, so kept myself to myself in my office, trying to distract myself with staffing budgets. Didn't work. I hadn't had butterflies for years but I got them walking to meet him; he was already there so I joined him. The conversation went from divorces into what he was doing now he was no longer married. He was often out on the town with his friends in Nottingham enjoying himself – I got a sense of him doing the Stephanie approach, to get over his wife leaving him. So this led me to ask him what he thought a single mum (well he knew and better to be open and honest) could do about meeting somebody new. Tripping the light fantastic wasn't really an option, I said. Again we skirted round the houses: you never know you might meet people through work, etc. Our lunch hour was drawing to a close and I still didn't really know how he felt, even though I sensed there was a sexual chemistry charging the atmosphere. But was he likely to take the next step? I wasn't sure but well we were in the nineties, surely it was OK for a woman to make a move – if for no other reason than I really needed to know.

I still remember it vividly today and wonder how on earth I did it. I moved the conversation on to the reality of the situation. I revealed that I had invited him to meet under false pretences; I wasn't really confused about the legal aspects of the divorce: I fancied him like crazy and needed to find a route to find out how he felt.

To my relief, he felt the same. He was really attracted to me but didn't know what to do about it either and was delighted I had told him. Oh my God we both felt the same – well I just wanted to kiss him – all those weeks of sexual chemistry building up. I couldn't – what if we were seen *and* the lunch hour was just about up. We quickly arranged that he would come round to mine for supper, after I had got Emily to bed, in two days' time.

How would I get through the next two days?

Well I didn't actually, I rang him the following day whilst at work. He was on a day off. I had forgotten he had temporarily moved back in with his parents, so I got his dad on the phone. I didn't know at the time, but Mark was actually seeing a girl also called Julie, so his dad just thought it was her. Mark came on the phone and I shared with him about my sleepless night and how I was feeling. In the end I suggested he came round that evening instead.

I put Emily to bed. I had prepared supper and was just about to sit on the sofa and wait for Mark, enjoying the moment that a really attractive man was coming to see me on a date – although not really a date as I had a small child. The phone rang and it was Steve, rabbiting on about how sorry he was and could we make a go of it and this and that – generally not making much sense as he had had a drink or two. Meanwhile Mark was lost and was trying to ring me and of course couldn't get through. I was thinking why is it again that Steve snatches away some of my enjoyment, even after he has gone? But in coaching we talk about deciding how to respond to an incident that arises. It is not others that cause the emotional response within us, it's how we choose to respond to what they have done.

So finally, getting rid of Steve and choosing to stay cheerful and excited, I went and poured myself a glass of wine. A knock at the door.

I opened it to find Mark with a bunch of flowers – cream tulips.

Cream tulips later became my wedding flowers. Yes, our romance blossomed and we are currently married with a son, William, as well as Emily.

Afternote

I think it is important for me to tell you what happened to Steve as it's sad and a story that might help others.

He managed to keep his drinking under control and he moved in with his sister and lived with her family in their front room for a while.

He managed to pull his life around but never really gave up the drinking as he never admitted to himself he had an issue. He bought himself a house, got another job. However despite remarrying and it looking like he had another chance of happiness, he still didn't really accept and deal with the alcohol.

Steve had had many significant events, I felt – losing me and Emily; losing his second wife; losing his job; being homeless on more than one occasion – but each time they seemed to send him further into his imaginary world. There were many times when he would ring to find out about Emily and he'd tell me about some adventure or story. They were never true but he believed them.

Steve died as a result of an accident. He fell down the stairs while under the influence of drink, at his mum's and he couldn't be resuscitated. He was too young to die and it was a waste of a life. I am no wiser about how to help alcoholics if they won't acknowledge their illness. It was truly sad that this young man's life had ended and that he'd not experienced the potential great things that had passed him by. Despite his problem, he was a lovely, kind and a gentle man, but obviously not strong enough to take life on and make the most of it for himself.

Another lesson for us all, make the most of every day, fill it with love, laughter and meaning. Make things happen for yourself and others, don't become a victim as Steve did.

Key areas of resilience demonstrated

Others have said to me that I demonstrated many characteristics and strengths going through what I did in connection with my model of resilience. The ones I would like to pull out are: self-efficacy, emotional self-control, clarity of purpose and future direction and support.

Self-efficacy

Self-efficacy was all about ultimately knowing I had what was needed to get through this. Despite the low points and being at time emotionally low, somewhere in me I knew I had what was needed. We all do, even if it's not evident to us at the time. Knowing this enabled me to sit down, once I was calmer, and work out another way forward to resolve the problem. I often used the phrase 'Well, it's down to me then'. In a peculiar way it helped remind me that I had the ability to control the way forward.

Emotional self-control

At times I was very calm and in control. Other times I was extremely angry, especially at Steve for not wanting to take control and move on from where he was. I was able to package my emotions and go to work. In fact work was a great help. It reminded me of normality, it took my mind off things, gave me things to achieve, which also helped my self-confidence.

There were times when the emotions took over, sadness at the situation, lots of frustration which tended to leave me in tears or angry. I read somewhere at the time, I think it was a coping mechanism for dealing with difficult children, that using your pillow to take out your anger and frustration was a way of getting all those negative emotions out – let's just say I needed a new pillow at the end of this.

Purpose

My key purpose was, at the time, to create a happy and supportive family which is why I think I invested so much energy into helping Steve. Getting the marriage and the family to work was important to me. This may not have been helpful in one aspect as it potentially kept me in a place of trying to fix Steve, which wasn't possible.

This sense of purpose got challenged after the bath incident and unconsciously at the time, as my values had been challenged, was replaced with a new one – being a mother and creating a safe and happy environment for my daughter to develop.

Support

Because I felt so isolated away from my family and friends, I knew I needed some professional help. Relate was that professional support, giving me time to reflect, see things from a different perspective and learn about me in that situation.

I also had support from my family and close friends when I just needed to recover and rebuild my reserves and energy. Being looked after by others during this time was extremely helpful, not having to make all the decisions and do everything for a change.

Work colleagues were also extremely helpful: having fun and laughter despite the difficulties: also knowing my situation helped me ask for things such as needing to leave early to sort out Emily, for example. Michelle the nanny was a fabulous support and created stability and love for Emily. Also the big help for me was knowing that Emily needed me to be a good mum, she was tiny and vulnerable so pouring lots of energy into her was rewarding in many ways and I'm sure a great help to me at this time.

Reminders for me through writing this chapter

- Believe in yourself. You are capable of more than you think.
- Do what you know/feels to be right, even if it's difficult.
- Take time for you so you can be the best you can be for others.

- Be forgiving of others. Let go of negative emotions and attachments. They aren't helpful and hold you back.

- Be curious about situations and things, especially about yourself. You'll be amazed what you discover.

Strategies to develop resilience

Self-efficacy

Watch the language you use, whether in talking to others or talking to yourself. 'I can't do this'; 'Why me?' – all take you back to a place of self-doubt and actually disempower you. If you feel like it is all too much and you feel you can't do something, just changing the words might not be enough, so find something you can do, break it down into small chunks, show yourself you can do something. Small chunks will enable you to make progress and reaffirm to yourself what you are capable of, helping to move towards the bigger solution.

The question, 'Why me?' which I did ask myself, just put me into the place of victim which is one of no power and others' fault. A better question is what is needed to help move you. 'How can I change this?'; 'What can I do to change this?'; 'What skills and talents can I pull on to help me at this time?' 'Who can help me?' – ask yourself the right type of question and your subconscious brain will find you an answer. It might not be immediately, but in time it will. Learning to ask powerful empowering questions of yourself is an important skill to learn.

Do it yourself. Take action. Take back control. This is a theme for many of the stories in this book. The women have done something which helps put them back in the driving seat where they feel in control again. When you feel in control, you feel you know what to do and it relieves lots of angst. However, I balance this with not doing everything and overloading yourself –ask for support.

Identify your bottom line. Identify the reasons for your repetitive pattern of behaviour which is not helpful. Where did it come from? How and when did it start? This was an area I worked on when in Relate around not asking for help and thinking I had to do it all. Once I was aware that there was a pattern and how it had developed, I was able to choose a different course of action. I'm not saying it was easy but that increased self-awareness was extremely enlightening and helped me be more conscious of what was going on.

Emotional self-control

Develop your Emotional Intelligence. Identify your strengths and development areas against the different facets. Emotional Intelligence is elastic. It can be enhanced and is a definite link to developing your resilience. We do EQi assessments and coaching with others and the results are really powerful. See our website for more information – www.naturescoaching.co.uk/emotional_intelligence2

Recognise when you are depleted, either overly tired, stressed or low, etc, as this is when you are most likely to lose control. You need to be tuned in to what your body and brain need regarding relaxation and taking time out. This leads me to the next tip:

Stop/Distract/Reflect

This is a simple technique that helps move people from reacting to situations to controlling their behaviour. Helping you choose how to react when something happens that would normally 'push your button' rather than just reacting.

My brother used to be great at knowing what buttons to push, the worst thing being that he's four years younger than me. It was only years later that I learnt to STOP myself, then DISTRACT myself with something else before choosing how to respond. Initially this takes time and might seem stilted but over time it speeds up. Often I say to clients, remove yourself from the situation that you know is emotionally charging you – going to the toilet is a great excuse – take deep breaths, go and notice something positive, such as a lovely view or a picture, feel yourself calm down, REFLECT calmly on the situation and then choose how you want to respond after reflecting objectively over the situation.

Reflecting on your emotionally charged situations is useful as it helps you to understand what it is that triggers that response.

THE ABC MODEL

A	B	C	D	E
Activating event/ situation	**Beliefs**	**Consequences**	**Dispute**	**Exchange**
– that you face	– thoughts and beliefs you hold about the situation	– behaviour exhibited internally and externally resulting from your beliefs	– beliefs and thoughts – are they rational or irrational?	– beliefs and thoughts into new balanced ones

The ABCDE exercise that follows can be applied to any areas of personal or professional life. We will be looking at the model slightly out of sequence, starting with A and then jumping to C, as this is the way it works best.

Activating event

When something upsetting happens, all sorts of raw emotions, thoughts and feelings run around in your head. You have an internal conversation with yourself about how to judge and evaluate the event. The ABCDE model helps you to separate the emotions you feel from the event itself, revealing your thought and belief patterns and helping you to replace unhelpful ones with a more positive approach.

Answer the following questions and write your responses down on a sheet of paper divided into columns ABCDE. You will need to allow plenty of room for detailed answers.

A = Activating event. Think of a recent situation that you felt frustrated and upset about.

It is important to be specific, eg, I had an argument with a work colleague.

Q1: What was the upsetting *situation*, known as the activating event or trigger?

Describe the actual event leading to the feelings of distress. Write it down in column A.

Emotions and thoughts

Also write down in column A your unhelpful negative feelings and the unpleasant automatic thoughts that preceded them. Again be specific.

Q2: What were your emotions: did you feel angry, upset, anxious, tearful?

Q3: What were the automatic thought(s) that preceded the emotion(s): what was going through your mind just before you started to feel this way? Eg: I should not be spoken to in this way. I feel useless.

Having completed part A (the activating event/trigger) we now go straight to C (the consequences).

Consequences

Q4: What were your behaviours (internal and external) that accompanied the activating event? We are looking for the consequences of the powerful combination of thoughts and emotions you were feeling.

For example:

Internally: red mist rising, increased heart rate, butterflies in your stomach, clenched fists.

Externally: angry and upset, you storm out of the room.

Write down what happened in column C:

Internally

Externally

Having completed parts A and C of the model, we move on to look at B (beliefs) and D (disputing them).

Beliefs

At this stage of the ABCDE model, it's not about the activating event (A) that leads to the consequences (C), but their beliefs (B) that trigger the negative automatic thoughts.

Beliefs are how an individual thinks and perceives a situation to be. It is their view of the world, as they see it and know it to be true, learnt from childhood experiences. If these beliefs are *irrational* rather than *rational*, they act as a trigger in producing recurring negative automatic thoughts. For example:

BELIEF: Everything I do must be perfect. If not, I am a failure.

Automatic thought: I am a failure.

Such rigid views and rules, particularly when unhelpful and distorted, generate high levels of stress and anxiety at the thought of failing. But the demand is impossible to achieve — no one is perfect.

We look next at how to dispute (D) beliefs and automatic thoughts (B).

Disputing the belief

For the purpose of the exercise, now read through the ten thinking distortions to see if you have used any of these styles in your activating incident. Then, using the examples provided under the D, start disputing them. Are they really true?

Over generalising, you come to a general conclusion based on a single piece of evidence or event. Ask yourself; am I over generalising, where are the facts to support my thinking?

Filtering when you filter you focus solely on the negative aspects of the situation and ignore the positive. Ask yourself if you are just looking at the negatives, what are the positives, what is a more balanced way of looking at the situation?

Magnifying, fearing the worst catastrophising the situation, exaggerating it to be worse than it really is. Good questions are; what is the worst that can happen, will this matter in a years time, what's the best things that can happen, what is good about this situation, what's most likely to happen?

All or nothing thinking, you think in black and white terms, right and wrong no middle ground. Ask yourself; is there another way of looking at this situation, what would grey look like rather than black and white, am I taking an extreme view, what would be a different perspective.

Disqualifying the positive, you reject the positive experiences by denying them and insisting they don't count. To help dispute this remember discounting the positive takes the joy out of your life and makes you feel inadequate, leaving one option - to accept the negative which is not helpful. You have a choice here allow the positive balance in.

Jumping to the wrong conclusions, making negative interpretations of other peoples thoughts, feelings and behaviors without any facts to support it. Great questions are; where's the evidence, how do you now what other people are thinking or that something awful will happen, what are you assuming about this and how can you check out those assumptions?

Labeling, where someone uses a label to call themselves or others, they call them names. Great questions to help dispute this are; where is the evidence to support the label, what are the labels preventing you from seeing, label the specific situation instead of yourself or others.

Emotional reasoning, this involves using your emotions as proof that things are the way they are, feelings are treated as fact. Ask yourself, where is the evidence to support your assumptions and intuitions.

Shoulds and musts, you are operating by rigid rules and allowing no room for flexibility, often implied by others rules often setting unrealistic expectations. The world is not set in stone, who is saying 'should' is that rule relevant for now, you have a choice what do you want rather than feeling you should?

Personalisation and blame, assuming responsibility for an event regardless of your actual impact on it, leading to guilt, shame and feelings of inadequacy. Questions; is this really all about you, where is the evidence it is your fault, what other explanations are there, are you really to blame?

Once you have disputed the belief you can exchange it for a more empowering and balanced one. One that is more helpful allowing you to move from this stuck position. This goes in column E.

Purpose and clarity of direction

Knowing what's really important to you in your life and having a hierarchy to these can be helpful. If you take my situation, I knew family — as in family unit of husband, wife and children — was really important to me. Thus the drive to 'fix it'. However, what came out was that Emily was more important than family. Identifying the things you won't compromise on, or looking at your values, is helpful, as if you're clear they will help guide you forward. Sometimes you might set a goal but won't make progress on it. Understanding your values, what's important to you, will help you sense check if the goal fits. Often it doesn't and that's why you're not making progress. Checking it against your list of values or what's important to you will help you set goals that fit. Once they do, you'll make progress.

Knowing what gets in the way of you achieving your goals.

We've spoken about values in the last point, but another blocker is fear. Knowing what you are fearful of helps you identify why you're not making progress. Understand the nature of the fear:

- Is it anticipating? Do you say, What if? Were you trying to predict the future in a way that stops you moving forward. It's good practice to consider what obstacles you might come across so you can anticipate and find solutions but not if you are using it as a prevention from moving forward.

- Is it irrational thinking, not based on fact, just your imagination running wild? Note it down and check it out objectively.

- Is it catastrophising, building things into the worst-case scenario?

- Is it rational, factual, actual?

Ways of dealing with your fears are to understand them. Acknowledge, share it with others, this often lessens the burden of it. Ask for help with it.

In Paul Hunting's book *Why Talk to a Guru When You Can Whisper to a Horse*, he describes fear as – Fantasy; Expectations; Appearing; Real – which I think is great. Fear is in our imagination, we don't know the future and often we build up fearful pictures that prevent us moving forward.

Letting go of the past. I am now tuned into hearing people say 'I should have'. At the time you most likely did the best you could do with the information and resources available to you. Beating yourself up continually by saying you should have is not helpful. We can't change our past but what we can do is change our relationship with it.

In connection with my relationship with Steve it was never going to be easy but I promised myself I would handle it with dignity and never 'bad mouth' him in front of Emily, so I didn't taint her views about him. I would always explain as best I could, understanding the age she was at the time, the truth in an objective way. To do this I had to let go of all those negative emotions I had about him. I became curious about alcoholism; learning more about it helped me understand more of his perspective rather than the hurt he created. Through this learning I was able to understand a more rounded picture of the situation. I didn't judge him. I accepted him for who he now was and I forgave him. I let it go into the past. It's not helpful to stay there. I had earlier in my life come across a woman whose husband had left her for another woman and 20 years on she was still angry and had all the hurt attached to when it initially occurred. She was living in the past and allowing herself to still be a victim.

At the time, I hadn't realised how powerful that insight was but one day it floated into my head and I thought I don't want to be miserable years hence because of what's happened. I want to be happy and have a fulfilled life. So I knew I just needed to let it go, hold no grudges or ill-feeling. Look at any old relationships you have with others that are negative and still full of emotions that won't enable you to let go and move on. A good way to understand this is to write down how you feel and explore why you are still holding on to it. Imagine what it would be like if you let it go? Build a future that is more encouraging and free from this negative hold. Decide to let it go. Sometimes setting fire to those negative emotions on the paper is quite symbolic of letting it go.

The Disney Technique. I shared with you the impact this had on me earlier in the book. This was developed by Walt Disney to aid the creative process when they were coming up with ideas to make a new story. He separates the 3 steps to effective brainstorming and planning, and critiquing the plan making sure they compliment each other rather than getting in the way. Often when we set out to think of new ideas we have either an inner critic or others working with us crtic it before its really been explored shutting down the thinking. This technique allows free thinking, planning and only critique around the plan not the idea.

Here is how you can use it, it is more effective working with someone else, however not impossible to use on yourself. This technique helps generate creative ideas and access your subconscious, as well as critiquing the plan, but not in a way that prevents true creative thinking.

Disney's Creative Planning

Three rooms/or three spaces

- [1] Dreamer room – dream up new ideas/projects/goals.
- [2] Realist – action-planning room where you devise a detailed business plan to bring the idea to fruition.
- [3] Critic – find flaws and weaknesses in the plan.

Background

- The process of creativity requires three key elements to be co-ordinated in order to create a well-formed idea: an idea, a plan and an edit of the plan.
- Robert Dilts devised an NLP technique on Disney's strategy by using spatial anchoring on the floor for the three parts

of the process, which he describes as Dreamer, Realist and Critic.

Exercise

Take your new idea for a project or just decide to dream openly and see what pops up.

- Select three physical locations on the floor and label them Dreamer, Realist and Critic. Place the latter away from the other two locations.
- Next, anchor the spaces:

  (a)   I want you to remember a time when you had a wonderful dream or were able to dream up or imagine new ideas without any inhibitions. I want you to step onto DREAMER location and relive that experience

  Think of a word to describe that experience.

  Step back off Dreamer.

  (b)   I want you to remember a time when you were able to think very realistically and were highly effective at planning. I want you to step onto the REALIST location and relive that experience.

  Think of a word to describe that experience.

  Step back off Realist.

  (c)   I want you to remember a time when you were able to constructively criticise a plan. I want you to step onto the CRITIC location and relive that experience.

  Think of a word to describe that situation.

  Step back off Critic.

- In the non-specific space ask: I want you to think of the goal/dream/outcome you want to achieve and when you are ready step onto the dreamer location. Use your cue word to help you remember that experience. Visualise yourself accomplishing this outcome and allow yourself to think about it in a free and uninhibited manner.

- Leave your dream of your outcome in that spot and step onto your realist location where you were your most resourceful planner. Now in your realist place put yourself into your dream. As you do this, I want you to see the process as if it were a storyboard or sequence of events and notice all the elements that are needed to make your dream become a reality.

- Leave your plan for your dream in that spot for now and step into your Critic location where you were your most useful constructive editor. Now in your Critic location find out if there is anything missing or needed from your Realist's plan. Check whether the plan seems achievable and realistic in the timescales. What might be other people's view on the plan? Then turn the criticisms into questions for the Realist.

- Move and negotiate between the second and third spaces until you feel you have an achievable plan that satisfies all parties. DO NOT CRITICISE THE DREAM AT ANY TIME.

  Take your questions back to your Realist location to see if the answers lie there.

  Take your questions back to your Dreamer location and see what creative help you can provide to answer these questions. Keep exploring in the various locations until you feel you have an idea, and a plan that has been well critiqued.

Support

Seek out professional support, whether that be counselling (which for me was through Relate), or a coach as I am now or any other trained individual. Coaching and counselling offers something different and it's important to understand what they offer so you know if it's what you need at that time.

Support from friends and family. Realise that you can't always do everything yourself and that others often want to help. For me I had to learn who to ask for what and not be put off when I asked for help, which took me ages to do so, if I didn't get it; I wasn't to be deterred from asking again.

Recognise who else needs support. Step out of your own issues and notice who else around you needs support. Offer it to them. It's great for taking you away from your issues, it helps add perspective on your life but, greater than that, it makes you feel good, which continues to build how you feel and your resources.

Sometimes you can be mutually helpful in your support as Stephanie and I were. We were both going through difficult times so, time out and laughter helped us both.

In order to succeed, people need a sense of self-efficacy, to struggle together with resilience to meet the inevitable obstacles and inequities of life. – Albert Bandura.

THE ACORNS OF RESILIENT GROWTH – A REMINDER

Self efficacy A person's belief about his or her ability and capacity to accomplish a task or to deal with the challenges of life. If your belief is high then this positively impacts on your confidence. People with high self efficacy tend to tackle problems, and persist for longer than those with low self efficacy. A person with high self efficacy will attribute failure to external factors rather than their ability. If you believe you can deal with the challenges you face and have confidence in your abilities then you can see how this will support resilience.

Optimism Hopefulness and confidence about the future and or the success of something. A tendency to expect the best possible outcome, the opposite being pessimists that tend only to see difficulty and challenges rather than opportunities. Keeping an optimistic view on what's in front of you that you have to deal with will help provide energy and possibility, which is important in developing your resilience.

Humour Is a state of mind an ability to appreciate and or express that which is humorous. For me it's about your ability to see the funny side of situations, especially around yourself, your ability to laugh. Which helps put things in to a different perspective, makes things less significant and enables you to refresh through laughter.

I found this insight into humour when researching which I think is great. "The term derives from the humoural medicine of the ancient Greeks, which taught that the balance of fluids in the human body, known as humours [Latin: *humor*, "body fluid"), control human health and emotion." Laughter releases lots of positive chemicals in to your body generating a feel good factor which supports a healthy life.

Emotional Self Control This is about your ability to understand your emotions and feelings and express them in a way that you are in control of. It's about acknowledging and recognising how you feel along side your ability share them with others that is not impulsive, explosive or you are not in control of. Being able to understand how we feel about certain aspects becomes enlightening and once aware then you know what you are dealing with, if something makes you sad acknowledge it, allow it to happen, don't try to suppress it, as it will not only impact on your health but also impact your ability to deal with the situation. Emotions are what makes us human tap into them and use them to help you acknowledge and then move forward through expressing them to yourself and others.

Purpose and clarity of direction The reason for you doing what you are doing, the 'why', the what's really important. Often linking to your personal values and often gives you a bigger connection to what you are doing in the moment. Where are you ultimately heading, what is it you seek? Having this clarity drives you through and makes things clear where you are going and helps you move beyond the immediate difficulty as you have strong reason to.

Problem solving, adaptability and having a growth mindset Having a growth mindset is about your belief that intelligence and talent can be developed and grown, the opposite of this is a fixed mindset which is a belief that intelligence is static, that you are born with your abilities and they can not be developed. If you have a growth mind set, which can be developed, you embrace change, persist despite obstacles, learn from feedback and criticism. Which often feeds your ability to be adaptable and creative in your problem solving, rather than to keep trying the same way to solve the problem. Being adaptable and trying new ways will help you find the right solution to your problem.

Perspective A mental view or outlook, a particular way of regarding something, a point of view. What I mean in connection with resilience is can you see things from a variety of perspectives, or are you fixed on seeing things from one place. It's the ability to open up your vision to see things from a number of positions. Can you stand back and look at things objectively that enables you to be open to other interpretations.

Once you can do this you get a more realistic interpretation on the situation rather than potentially your narrow dimension.

Support There are three different aspects to this; your ability to support and be kind and compassionate to yourself, your ability to ask for support and help from others when you need it and your ability to see others difficulties and offer support. The literal definition is 'a thing that bears the weight of something or keeps it upright'. What do you need to help you to keep upright and function well? How good are you at helping yourself, are you kind and supportive or are you overly hard, is that internal voice sabotaging your abilities and potential to succeed?

Do you look after yourself in the health and wellbeing aspects, do you exercise, eat well and rest? Or do you live life constantly on the go don't nourish yourself either nutritionally or spiritually. Our bodies need down time and like nature need the right nutrients from our food. Exercise also nourishes and lifts help us see things from a different perspective, as does taking regular time out.

Supporting others, are you so tied up in your own difficulties that you don't see other people suffering or having difficulties? Taking yourself away from your own challenges and focusing on others and then seeing how you can help them support your resilience on a numerous levels. It removes you from your world, which will temporarily remove you from the angst and stress, it helps you see things from different perspectives, it will refresh you and support you ability to problems solve differently. However the biggest element is that we are more fulfilled through supporting and helping others than we realise. It gives us a real sense of satisfaction and enjoyment.

There is lots of research out about the positive impact of random acts of kindness. Give it a go and notice the positive impact it has on how you feel.

How do you rate yourself against the eight acorns?

Acorn	Rating out of 10 when 1 is terrible and 10 is consistently good	What would increase your score by 1-2 points?	What exactly are you going to do?
Self efficacy			
Optimism			
Humour			
Emotional self control			
Purpose and clarity of direction			
Problem solving, adaptability and growth mindset			
Perspective			

Support - Self - Others - Asking for help			

Summary

Through reading this book I hope you have been inspired by the amazing women who have kindly shared their stories. All of us are normal, everyday women who happen to have had a few things in our life that have been difficult or challenging; or we have just wanted to improve and develop ourselves, but found it difficult. We have all wanted to share our experiences in the hope that between us we connect with other women who may also be going through some challenging times. Hopefully, through reading about our stories, we have shown you how things are possible and what difficulties and challenges can be overcome.

We hope that you will develop your resilience through trying some of the ideas suggested in developing the various elements. Working on these while you're feeling good about them is a great place to start. Don't wait for a difficulty when your resilience is challenged – work on them now and 'be prepared' as I was taught through my time as a Brownie and Girl Guide.

Enjoy exploring new ways to develop yourself; who knows what new opportunities may open up for you through working on yourself. Developing your resilience will enable you to achieve more of what you want in your life.

I would love to hear from you about what has worked, what you enjoyed or if you want to share your story for others. Please let me know through the website – www.treeofresilience.com or www.naturescoaching.co.uk

Thank you

To the women in this book who I've had the pleasure of knowing and learning about their lives and for trusting me to write their stories.

Thank you for being prepared to share those stories in this book for others to be able to read.

To my supporters and helpers who have encouraged me and for some who have actively helped in the early stages, Dorothy especially.

To my clients who are always a pleasure to work with and continually develop me through working with them.

To my family who have supported me through my various difficulties and shared in the good moments too. I love you all.

To my friends who in their different ways have encouraged me and shared some fun moments together.

To the many people I have been privileged to learn from through my developmental journey: Bev James, Nancy Kline, Bridget Grenville-Cleave, and all my fellow coaches.

> *The best years of your life are the ones in which you decide your problems are your own. You do not blame them on your mother, the ecology, or the president. You realise that you control your own destiny.* – Albert Ellis.

www.treeofresilience.com

Notes

Notes

Notes